Talkin' 'Bout My Generation

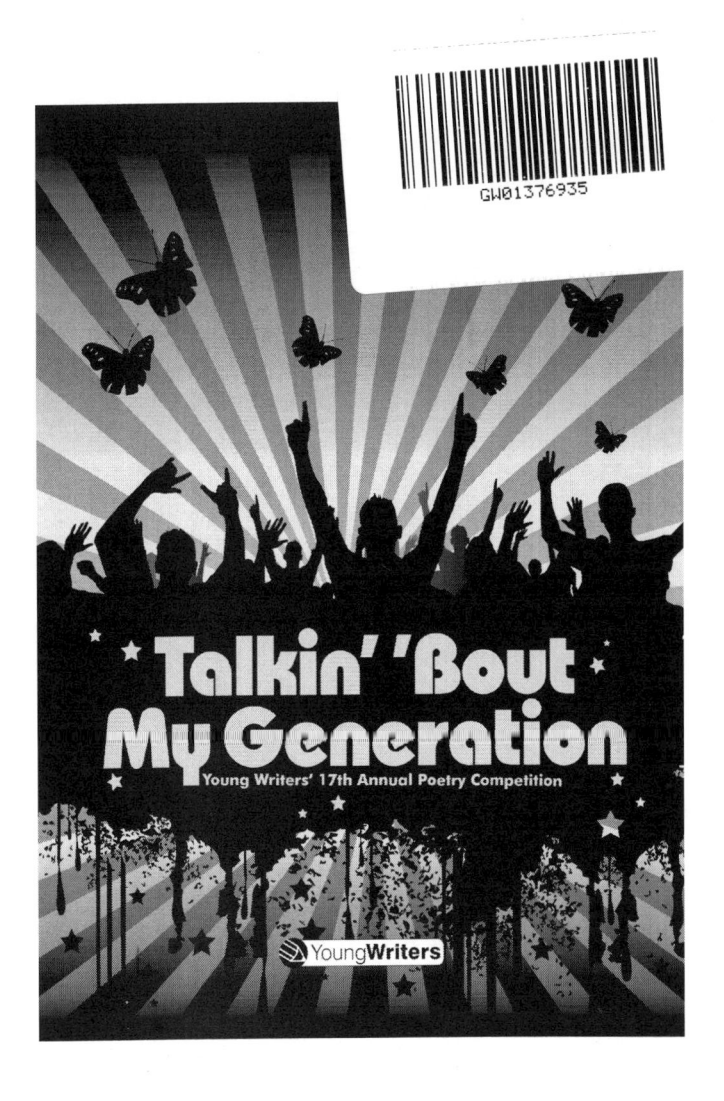

Young Writers' 17th Annual Poetry Competition

Poems From The West Country
Edited by Mark Richardson

Young Writers

First published in Great Britain in 2008 by:
Young Writers
Remus House
Coltsfoot Drive
Peterborough
PE2 9JX
Telephone: 01733 890066
Website: www.youngwriters.co.uk

All Rights Reserved

© Copyright Contributors 2007

SB ISBN 978-1 84431 470 6

Foreword

This year, the Young Writers' *Talkin' 'Bout My Generation* competition proudly presents a showcase of the best poetic talent selected from thousands of up-and-coming writers nationwide.

Young Writers was established in 1991 to promote the reading and writing of poetry within schools and to the young of today. Our books nurture and inspire confidence in the ability of young writers and provide a snapshot of poems written in schools and at home by budding poets of the future.

The thought, effort, imagination and hard work put into each poem impressed us all and the task of selecting poems was a difficult but nevertheless enjoyable experience.

We hope you are as pleased as we are with the final selection and that you and your family continue to be entertained with *Talkin' 'Bout My Generation Poems From The West Country* for many years to come.

Contents

Ansford School, Castle Cary
    Poppy Cole (11)   1
    Chloe Sage (11)   1
    Jo Keating (11)   2
    Jade Crombie (11)   3
    Indigo Hayes (12)   4
    Harry Tabor (11)   4
    Florentino Monteiro (11)   5
    Fraser House (11)   5
    Ellie Gore (11)   6
    Bethany-Eleanor Sugg (12)   7
    Joel Batchelor (12)   8
    Imogen Millington (12)   9
    Caroline Bennett (11)   10
    Daisy Searle (12)   11
    Jasmine Badman (11)   12
    Sarah Evans (11)   13

Balcarras School, Cheltenham
    Ellie Daxter (13)   13
    Hannah Churchill (13)   14
    William Evans (13)   15
    Naomi Edwards (13)   16
    Elliot Bishop (13)   17
    Estelle Dyer (13)   18
    Jake Flower (13)   19
    Abi Sheridan (13)   20
    Hannah McCarthy (14)   21
    Sara Paterson (13)   22
    Chris Parker (14)   22
    Rosemary Wallis (15)   23
    Claire Collier (15)   24
    Megan Reid (13)   25
    Grace Harris (13)   26
    Adele Toyne (15)   26
    Todd Tyler (13)   27
    Natalie O'Meara (15)   28
    Mark Whistler (13)   29
    Tabitha Robinson-Wall (14)   30

Danni Coughlan (15) ... 31
Chloe Mortimer-Stokes (13) ... 32
Frances Burton (15) ... 33
James Gandhi (14) ... 34
Alice Brookes (15) ... 35
Jenny Lewis (13) ... 36
Joe Trigg (16) ... 37
Chris Folland (15) ... 38
Jess Powell (15) ... 39

Bredon School, Tewkesbury
Jake Martin (15) ... 39

Colston's Girls' School, Bristol
Emma Galton (13) ... 40
Aaghna Patel (11) ... 40
Ellie Lawrence (13) ... 41
Rebecca Bailey (13) ... 41
Savannah Sevenzo (13) ... 42
Martha Wood (12) ... 43
Katie Crowley (12) ... 44
Laura Price (12) ... 45
Ayanna Sharp (13) ... 46
Ocean Murphy (13) ... 46
Elske Waite (14) ... 47
Florence King (12) ... 48
Charlotte Rutter (14) ... 48
Reema Mobeireek (11) ... 49
Emma Hennessey (12) ... 49
Gillian Browne (14) ... 50
Miranda Sadler (12) ... 51
Jess Purcell (12) ... 52
Emily Wright (11) ... 53
Charlotte Lacey (12) ... 54
Alice Stockwell (12) ... 54
Eve Miller (12) ... 55
Chloe Campbell (12) ... 55
Ellena Murphy ... 56
Charlotte Fletcher (13) ... 56
Frances Murphy (11) ... 57
Kimberley Jones (13) ... 58

Evleen Price (12)	59
Alexandra Denny (11)	60
Mariam Olatidoye (12)	61
Katie Smith (12)	62
Sophia Doughty (12)	62
Hannah Cullum (12)	63
Lois Linter (12)	63
Alisha Litt (12)	64
Anmol Anjam (12)	65
Lydia Barnes (12)	66
Mattie Ward (13)	67
Kate Brennan (12)	68
Anna Lawrence (11)	69
Rose Juliet (12)	70
Ruth Walker	71
Isabelle Craner (11)	72
Daisy Miller (11)	73
Ayla Norman (11)	74
Meg Lawrence (12)	75

Downend School, Bristol

Amy Hillier (12)	75

Hayesfield School, Bath

Katriona Pierce (12)	76
Olivia De Miceli (12)	77
Bethany Stenning (12)	77
Bryony Parsons (12)	78
Melissa Pope (13)	79
Tillie Jarvis (12)	79
Jessica Clothier (12)	80
Ellie Frank (12)	81
Emily Appleby-Matthews (12)	82
Amber Harrup (12)	82
Sophie Gwilt (12)	83
Alissa Tooley (12)	83
Isabel Williams (12)	84
Charlotte Imianowski (13)	85
Sashia Webb-Hayward (12)	86
Lauren Schofield (13)	87
Bethany Mitchell (13)	88

Bethany Davison (12)	89
Chloë Meanwell (12)	90
Megan Hazell (13)	90
Imogen Ely (12)	91
Kirsty Smith (13)	91
Bethany Walls (12)	92
Maddie Dawes (13)	93
Alice Ware (13)	93
Chelsea Buchan (13)	94
Emma Park (12)	94
Lily Jennings (13)	95
Lucy Bean (12)	96
Sedona Ferguson (13)	97

Minehead Middle School, Minehead

Tom Hawkins (12)	98
Rayne Holland-Smith (12)	98
Alysha Kendall (12)	99
Dan Farmer (12)	99
Elsie Berry (12)	100
Francesca Broome (11)	101
Gabriella Routley (12)	102
Callum Langley (12)	102
Jessie Evans (12)	103
Viki Jones (12)	103
Jonathan Leary-Hemans (12)	104
Daniel Thompson (12)	105
Charlie Tudball (12)	106
Jade de Ste Croix (12)	106
Leanne White (12)	107
Sam Fox (12)	107
Luke Cutler (12)	108
Algene Gascon (12)	108
Jacob Jordan (13)	109
Tom Reed (12)	109
Abbie Webber (12)	110
Tom Coward (12)	110
Ciaran Barker (11)	111
Gracie Legg (11)	111
Katie Beauchamp (13)	112

Jess Lovegrove (12)	112
Joshua Chilcott (11)	113
Lea Blackford (12)	113
Kyran Wilkins (12)	114
Michael Graddon (12)	114
Sam Small (13)	115
Thomas Strachan (12)	115
Scott Gurnett (12)	116
Charlotte Williams (12)	116
Rebecca Willmetts (12)	117
William Daughtrey (11)	117
Thomas Clegg (11)	118
Hamish Cuthbertson (11)	118
Richie Lethaby (11)	119
Bosko Reynolds (11)	119
Samuel Sparks (11)	120
Tara Howard (11)	120
Abigail Smith (12)	121
Charlene Kendall (12)	121
Luke Senior (11)	122
Sarah Clegg (11)	122
Billy Stove (11)	123
Jessica Griffiths (11)	123
Josh Law (13)	124
Bethany Hobbs (11)	124
Jake Thompsett (11)	125
Kieran Williams-Carr (11)	125
Sophie Morton (11)	126
Toby Kerslake (11)	126
Hannah Norman (11)	127
Danimay Palmer (10)	127
Sophie Coates (11)	128
Brandon Scarlett (11)	128
Reem Nicholls (11)	129
Ellie-May Murphy (11)	129
Jack Thake (13)	129

St John's School & Community College, Marlborough

Frances Hamblin (12)	130
Ruby Tucker (12)	131

St Katherine's School, Bristol
    Hannah Beard (13)   132

The Crypt School, Gloucester
    Ben Harris (14)   133
    James Weaver (14)   133
    Ryan Dunne (14)   134
    Bradley Pring (14)   134
    Ben Dowd (14)   135
    Chris Silk (14)   135
    Ben Simmonds (12)   136
    Josh Myrans (14)   136
    Liam Ward (14)   137
    Christian Lange (14)   137
    Phil Morgan (15)   138
    Luke Wildman (11)   138
    Jack Ashton (11)   138
    Mike Smith (12)   139
    Dan Bannister (14)   139
    Dane Nash (11)   140
    Charlie Williams (11)   140
    Daniel Charlton (11)   141
    Adam Crabbe (12)   141
    Adam Allen (11)   142
    Max Williams (11)   142
    Jordan Hopwood (11)   142
    Matthew Hunter (12)   143
    Edward Plant (11)   143
    Harry McDowell (12)   144
    Matthew Wilkinson (11)   144
    Tom Beckett (11)   144
    James Robertson (17)   145
    Theo Tibbs (11)   145
    Josh Downham (11)   146
    Marty Fisk (11)   146
    Ben Gribble (13)   147
    Liam Walsh (12)   147
    Leigh Smith (12)   148
    Josh Williams (12)   148
    Katie Wedgbury (16)   149
    James Clifford (15)   149

Bradley Meredith (12)	150
Mike Payne (12)	150
Aaron Smith (12)	151
James Stevens (12)	152
Ben Rhodes (14)	153
Tim Smith (12)	154

The High School for Girls, Gloucester

Adele Franghiadi (11)	154
Renee James-Bryan (12)	155
Freya Hansen (11)	156
Samantha Collins (11)	157

West Somerset Community College, Minehead

Harry Rogers (13)	157
Dawn-Marie Williams (13)	158
Alice O'Shea (13)	159
Charley Chandler	159
Emilie Smith (14)	160
Oliver Bartle (13)	160
Eleanor Stone (15)	161
Davey Owen	161
Remi Toth (14)	162
Grace Wilson (13)	162
Francesca Walker (14)	163
Kieran Parsons (14)	163
Rebecca Salter (14)	164
Nancy McGowan (13)	164
Abbie Davies (14)	165
Steff Hartgen (14)	165
Amie Hutchings (13)	166
Jack Sully	166
Finlay Bastable	167
Stephen Yard (13)	168
Kayleigh Kendall (13)	168
Joe Stileman (14)	169
Clare Davey (13)	169
Jake Dorrill (14)	170
Briony Flello	171
Abi Owen (14)	172
Beth Goodwill (14)	172

Emily Townsend (14)	173
Michelle Saunders	174
Nick Hosegood (14)	175
Jacob Cammidge	176
Connor Murphy (13)	176
Harry Mouzouri	177
Greg Wood (13)	177
Dean Manley (13)	178
Bradley Price (13)	178
Ryan Lewis & Jack Coward	179
Christina Le Rendu	179
Joe Francis	180
Annie Rowling	181
Katherine Peeks (14)	182
Faye Wolley (13)	183
Eleanor Facey (13)	184

The Poems

Giraffe

The giraffe stands alone,
He looks lonely,
Poor him,
I wish I could help him,
But I can't get a giraffe.

The giraffe looks proud,
She looks like she's achieved something,
Lucky her,
I wish I could be like her,
But I am not a giraffe.

The giraffe looks upset,
He looks like he's been picked on,
Poor him,
I wish I could comfort him,
But I can't speak to a giraffe.

Poppy Cole (11)
Ansford School, Castle Cary

The Last Generation

What is the world going to turn out to be,
The generation for you and me,
The animals are dying under the sun,
Gradually, hurtfully, one by one,
The plants are dying with the fish in the sea,
This is called pollution, it happens gradually,
They chat about global warming, I don't have a clue,
How do I help? There's nothing to do.

One day I will find what is in my mind,
I blame the last generation!

Chloe Sage (11)
Ansford School, Castle Cary

They Don't Listen

They don't listen to our ideas
They think it's a kind of joke
Ha, ha. I'm not laughing
Even when we say an idea
They just take all the limelight away from us.

We could change the world
Ideas on global warming, pollution
But they don't care
We just sit in the corner
With the little jobs that do not matter.

We have to live on their ideas
Breathing, sleeping, eating
But we have better ones
They do not count
Just silly and strange
Not meaning a thing.

Us children
We can rule the country
But no one will let us
Because we are non existent to them.

The adults aren't really the best
It's us the children that count
We are the generation of the future
We are the future.

Jo Keating (11)
Ansford School, Castle Cary

The World As It Is

Have you ever wondered why people do things?
Why do people smoke, drink or do drugs?
The world is a strange place, full of love and hate,
From the Great Wall of China to the Eiffel Tower.

Why do people go to jail?
Was it murder, abuse or stealing?
From chavs, emos and killers,
Deep down we are all the same.

Why do people drink underaged?
Are they depressed or mad?
Drugs make people do stupid things,
What would we do without help?

Why do people break promises?
Do you love or hate?
Are you in it for the money?
Or are you real and true?

Why do people make fun of thin and fat?
Is size zero really the best?
Or is size 25? What's right?
Neither are good, but we can help that.

Is the world different?
Or are we the same?
Just think of the world as it is,
As it is today.

Jade Crombie (11)
Ansford School, Castle Cary

Us

We're neither old and grey
Nor young and colourful!
We're us.

Your contribution
Global warming and pollution!
Not us, that's you.

We look to the future
But never the past!
We're us.

A life of regret
And broken promises!
Not us, that's you.

Can't you see this world is ours not yours!

Indigo Hayes (12)
Ansford School, Castle Cary

The War

I am a young war child
It's loud
It's dark
People are dying
Arrows flying
Prime minister lying.

People frightened
People running
Bombs lighting up the night sky
Innocent people screaming
Innocent people dying.

Harry Tabor (11)
Ansford School, Castle Cary

Abandoned Animals

Waiting for someone to take me.
Feeling alone.
Asking for help
But no one responds.

I'm so sad.
I can't hold it anymore.
I miss my family.
My heart is torn.

I don't know what to do,
I'm freezing, but I still have my toy,
I'm going to hug it close to my heart,
I'm going home to see what's going on.

Why did they leave me?
Are they missing me?
I don't know . . .
But I miss my family.

Florentino Monteiro (11)
Ansford School, Castle Cary

The Thing

The roar of the engine
As it gallops down the road.
The purring of the engine
As it pounces into gear.
Faster and faster,
Until it goes out of sight.
Crash, he smashes,
He collides with a car,
Both drivers are killed.
So why should we drink and drive?

Fraser House (11)
Ansford School, Castle Cary

Corridor Rush

The bell starts ringing,
But I dread to leave the classroom.
I dread to see the sea of people,
Budge straight past me.

The Year Elevens get their way,
Shouting to their friends.
All the different ties,
Like they're trying to set trends.

The year sevens, (that's me),
Get pushed up to the wall,
I can see the end but I can't get past,
I'm *stuck!*

Scared now,
Gum sticking,
Late for class,
No one cares,
Never get free,
Detention for life!

But now the rush is dying,
There was no need crying,
I'm free . . .

For 50 minutes!

Ellie Gore (11)
Ansford School, Castle Cary

The Ultimate Perspective Of The World

The ultimate perspective of the world,
Is that people never do what they're told.

Somehow,

Life goes to pot if you haven't got a frock
or a packet of ciggies in your pocket.

Somehow,

If you haven't got the fashion,
there's no need for passion,
No one cares, no one knows, that's life.

Somehow,

People get put into blinding groups,
mocha, emo, chav,
can't people see, they're being told who to be?
Mocha, emo, chav.

But,

Life is about the individual,
so don't be boring and follow a ritual.

I'm talking to you! My generation!
For confidence is the key,
To getting where you want to be.

Bethany-Eleanor Sugg (12)
Ansford School, Castle Cary

My Mad, Future World

Just think of a world
where the rich are poor,
and the poor are rich,
there's no slaves anymore.

There's no more politics,
and no more war,
there's no more hunters
to kill all the boar.

There's no good or bad,
there's no bad or good,
and there's no more myths
of a killer in a hood.

All the adults are short,
all the kids are tall,
all the babies are big
and all the oldies are small.

This world has transformed,
through a period of time,
it was 2007
when I started this rhyme.

Joel Batchelor (12)
Ansford School, Castle Cary

We All Fall Down

The grisly violence,
Then, sudden, deathly silence,
It can only mean one thing,
It's all about to begin,
We all fall down.

Two buildings fall down, it's a big deal,
But what do I feel,
For those people inside?
I wish I'd never lied,
We all fall down.

Crashing through,
Like it's going through you,
I've seen it all before,
But never from the floor,
We all fall down.

Digging deeper, just to find
I'm not the only one with things on my mind,
The past will last,
So run, run, run fast,
Yes, we all fall down.

Imogen Millington (12)
Ansford School, Castle Cary

The Sunrise

A silent whip,
cracks through the horizon,
parting the dark night,
a burning hole,
getting bigger and bigger
as it creeps into the sky to form day.

A rainbow of colours
takes over the sky.
Then a fanfare of birds
sing their opening line,
tweeting and cooing,
calling, in time.

The world wakes up,
and the noise begins,
chattering, nattering and clattering.
The appreciation of sunrise
falls silent again
and waits for the next time,
as it will happen again and again.
It goes on forever.

Caroline Bennett (11)
Ansford School, Castle Cary

No Feelings

The world is nothing to me,
Black, dark and dead.
I have no feelings about things,
They are in my head.

I cannot express my thoughts,
I cannot talk to you.
I cannot run away,
I can't get to the loo.

As I lie in my bed,
I have no idea,
That people are dying in Iran,
Children disappear.

I can do nothing to help,
I can do nothing to please,
I wish I could speak,
I wish I could sneeze.

But I can't because my world is black,
My world is dark,
My world is dead.

Daisy Searle (12)
Ansford School, Castle Cary

Black And White

Imagine a checkerboard.

People say,
That your colour does matter,
Your age, your height
And whether you're thinner or fatter.

The colour of your hair,
The shape of your eyes,
All equals up
To tears and sighs.

Black and white, black and white, black and white . . .

But we know why they do it,
There's no need to cry,
Deep down inside
We all know why.

Black and white, black and white, black and white . . .

Honestly, guys,
We need to get along,
Stand all together
And stay standing strong.

It's really not big,
To make fun of someone's face,
Neither their name, hairstyle,
Learning rate or race.

Black and white, black and white, black and white . . .

Jasmine Badman (11)
Ansford School, Castle Cary

Mistreated

Am I meant to be?
Everywhere I look I see sadness
My parents hurt me - my world of pain
Big, black bruises down my arms and back
I feel like a person with no soul
I'm broken - not all there
No one understands
My dear, beloved friends don't know what's going on
As I sit in my bedroom, the only place where I feel I belong,
I'm invisible
I hear shouting, screaming, my mum and dad are fighting again
Still after all that, they take their anger out on me
I'm scared
The only thing to comfort me is my solemn bear!

Sarah Evans (11)
Ansford School, Castle Cary

Wartime Sacrifices

The sharp, quick stund of failed heroes
Failure thrust upon them unwillingly
The equal nameless units that were near those
And their loved ones, lost their pride and joy completely
A name read off a list is all to mourn them
A gruff and pompous voice is all we hear
Although they were taken far away
We know they'll fill our souls and will be near
Their final wakening in the rancid trenches
The crisp winter ground, soft and cushioned too
The haunting flashbacks of their final retches
Their hearts lay cold, once warm through and through
The twisted, selfish opinions of the man
By once believing that no one could hurt me
War sets in stone the proof that people can.

Ellie Baxter (13)
Balcarras School, Cheltenham

My War Poem

War.
Men march to war,
Knowing the problems they'll face.
Losing their family,
Losing themselves.

The unwanted, deadly gas
That slowly limits their breathing.
Blood that pushes up through their lungs,
Becoming unstoppable.

Watching your one friend,
Your brother, walk towards the light,
As a bright and 'beautiful' bullet catches him.
Know you're inches away from being just like him.

The lush green field now covered with red marks,
Where each valuable soldier
Once risked his life for peace.
But it never came. Not before. Not after.

People at home try to pray for them,
But it can't stop the war.
Just a waste of time,
A waste of breath.

As for the good things,
Well, there's plenty of them.
Just as long as the little bird sings
And my life is like a precious gem.

Hannah Churchill (13)
Balcarras School, Cheltenham

A Waste Of Death

The clatter of gunfire,
Sentencing an innocent man's life.
Not thought for his family,
His children, his wife.
As he fell to the floor,
He pondered on why,
When there's thousands of soldiers
He should be the one to die.

He lay on the ground, with nothing left,
His life, simply, a waste of death.

Blood trickled down,
From his cold, cold heart.
To think that tomorrow
He'd be slumped into a cart
And wheeled off to the graveyard
For his final burial.
Seen off by soldiers,
Only there for the free meal.

The end of his life, he lost.
His life, simply a waste of death

He feared the embarrassment,
The shame that came with dying.
But since he would be dead,
What's the use in trying?

And as he draws his final breath.
His life, simply a waste of death.

William Evans (13)
Balcarras School, Cheltenham

My Poem - Generation

The world is big and round
Bigger than a pound
With lots of money
To fill your tummy
But the money doesn't get around

People in the world
Are starving all the time
They haven't got a dime
So they resort to crime

They fight with fists
They fight with guns
That's what some people become
Just to get some money
To feed their hungry tummies

The world is big and round
Bigger than a pound
With lots of money to feed people's tummies
But the money doesn't get around.

Naomi Edwards (13)
Balcarras School, Cheltenham

My Generation - Sad Poem

Happy times come,
Happy times go,
When you're happy,
Everyone knows,
Through good or bad,
Happy or sad,
Happiness is the best friend
I've never had.

Some people think happiness is everywhere,
But I think there is none of it,
Look around, it's not anywhere,
In no one's hearts a little bit.

Happy times come,
Happy times go,
When you're happy,
Everyone knows,
Through good or bad,
Happy or sad,
Happiness is the best friend
I've never had.

Elliot Bishop (13)
Balcarras School, Cheltenham

Animal Cruelty

Animals wander around the town,
Passing diseases when they're let down.
Farmers' earnings are destroyed,
As the 'higher status' gets annoyed.
Bird flu lingers in the cattle,
Is it the everlasting battle?

A dog or cat can be a best friend,
On whose love you can always depend.
When you're feeling sad and sometimes alone,
A lick on the cheek and the award of a bone.
I count my blessings and feel full of pride,
When I stroke my furry friend by my side.

Animals create a lot of mess,
People around get distressed.
Animals are tragically abused,
But who is accused?
Their owners are often the ones to neglect,
But animals should also have our respect.

Estelle Dyer (13)

The War That Never Ends

The war we fight, each morning dawn,
Brings a harsh, hollow way of life that cries for mourn.
In coffins lie those strong, innocent and dead,
Whilst the terrorist monsters safely lie in bed.

9/11 drew the last straw;
leaving the whole world full of shock and forlorn.
The civilisation of the Third World gone, hit down, shot down,
with the universe torn.
Terrorism shocks, the world full of dread,
With guns, bombs and even words, we fled.

The terrorist attack continues to show,
With the world's morale at an all-time low.
Fear strikes when crossing the street,
In case attacks we continue to meet.
The young, the innocent, the newborn, soon dead,
Get rid of the monsters; let us lie simply,
safely, soulfully in bed.

Jake Flower (13)
Balcarras School, Cheltenham

The Future Generation

They tell us off for messy rooms,
When all the time their problem looms,
What have they done to a world so sweet?
The world they filled with cars and concrete,
Where pollution is a dilemma faced every day,
But now I ask you, who will pay?
It is the men who made the mess,
Or will they get off with less?

Is it us, who has to fix it?
Will our elders merely quit it?
The disaster that they created,
They just waited and waited and waited,
Until someday, we'd grown up,
Shouting, arguing, constant tut, tut, tut.
When all of that is finished and done,
They say, 'Could you help us, hun?'

How to solve it? Is all we say,
'Don't be under forty, not by a day,'
So we have to fix a mess we didn't make,
Because of all your silly mistaken,
You will die of natural causes,
Because none of you ever pauses,
We will die by your doing,
Because you just kept on ruining.

Abi Sheridan (13)
Balcarras School, Cheltenham

Another Soldier Dead

His best friend dying at his feet
While he sits there with nothing to eat

'No, please, save him!'
'I'm sorry, he's gone.'
And it's all because of that damned bomb,
'we've got a war to fight,
so leave him, come on.'
he said goodbye and walked away,
he said he'd fight, come what may.

He from there and forever on,
Praying his way through, with his friend long gone.
Of course it was still hard,
Sometimes terrifying,
Like bubbles, floating through the air,
Everywhere bombs, still flying.
It only takes one, just one bomb
To kill this soldier dead.
It only takes one, just one bomb
To kill another dead.
It only takes one, just one bomb
To make the fields turn red.

Slowly, as he was dying,
He smiled, as he said,
'It only takes one, just one bomb
to kill this soldier, dead.'

Hannah McCarthy (14)
Balcarras School, Cheltenham

My War Poem

The floor of the trenches, very springy
Dead men buried, so the floor feels pingy.
Yet all my friends are fading away
I wish I could just go home and play.

Soldiers slowly running short
Another boat arrives in port.
Lots of people have perished from this
As the battle keeps to persist.

Listening to the guns
Killing all my friends
The bullets weigh a ton
I'm looking forward to when the war ends.

Lots of men missing their families
Their loved ones in great agony
When the war ends
I hope I will, go home again.

Sara Paterson (13)
Balcarras School, Cheltenham

My Generation

Gulp, gulp, gulp, goes the sound of booze
Smoking cigarettes in the middle of the loos.
Getting into fights in the middle of the street
There's nothing to do but retreat.

Burglary and robbing everywhere
All you can do is stop and stare.
Things are stolen all the time
Police are trying to stop the crime.

People taking drugs in the clubs
Dropping their cigarette stubs.
Trying to cut down,
But they're gonna drown.

Chris Parker (14)
Balcarras School, Cheltenham

The System

The computer screen
Flashes before my eyes
As I try
To concentrate on a cultural poem
And forget about life itself

Whatever happened to laughing?
Where did that joyous sound go?
As I walk these empty, gloomy corridors
All I hear is the clattering of feet
On the hard stone floor

What kind of life is this?
Where we are not allowed to live?
Talking, smiling
Not allowed
As the powerful keep us down

Treated like robots
From a tender age
Moulded into their perfect children
Throughout the day
No mood for fun
Just work
From morning to night.
In hope of a much deserved pass

But then what?
What happens next?
Once you've got these much needed grades
Where do these robots go?
Once they're spat out of the system
Left to wander the streets
And ponder what they should do.

When I see these people
I can't help asking myself why they even do it
Why do they put themselves through it
And more importantly why do their parents let them?

Rosemary Wallis (15)
Balcarras School, Cheltenham

Nobody Cares

We used to be weak,
Couldn't stand death.
We were afraid of stepping out
And never going back.

But the screams of men
Have toughened our hearts
We knew we wouldn't survive,
And now nobody cares.

The rats ran wild
As they fed off the dead.
Vermin spread,
It crept through our beds.

Many men went out
Never to return.
Bodies lay forgotten
They never knew peace.

The roar of guns
Shattered the still, night air.
But we didn't listen
And it never ends.

But here we lie
Lost and forgotten;
We are the forgotten souls
Of a cold, dead war.

Our bodies sunk
In the muddy lands.
Many lie there
Never to be whole.

We will never know life
As it could have been;
The gentle touch of loved ones,
And the laughter of the young.

All that we can hear
Is the roar of those guns,
The screams of innocent men.
We don't remember love.

We did it for our country
For honour and truth.
But we didn't survive
And nobody cares.

Claire Collier (15)
Balcarras School, Cheltenham

Music

The base of a new generation
It comes from the heart
In the home of the nation
Is where the music starts

Music frees the human soul
Inspires men of power
To stop suffering and help the poor
And change upon the hour

Though people don't agree sometimes
The music doesn't play
They don't see what's in our minds
There's nothing left to say

When the world is at war
I'm deaf, blind and paralysed
Because the Earth is so sore
When the music dies, so do I.

Megan Reid (13)
Balcarras School, Cheltenham

My Generation

My generation is full of news
People have opinions, people have views
Some are good, some are bad
Most make politicians mad
Politicians think they're right
In the Commons room they fight
Over life, over war
Most don't care, so give a yawn

If they did, they'd see the things
You hear on the news or when the phone rings
If there's one thing they should learn
It's how to speak when it's their turn
If they did these things well
They would feel real swell
Until they see the world's a scare
People like them everywhere.

Grace Harris (13)
Balcarras School, Cheltenham

Life . . .

Can't see the world through a bamboo tube,
Can't see the sea through a message in a bottle.

Can't live life like a bird,
Can't be free.

Can't leave it all behind,
Can't leave the strings and ties of our lives.

Trapped like a bird in a cage,
But at least the cage is home.

Adele Toyne (15)
Balcarras School, Cheltenham

Street Girl

My heart is thumping with fierce fear
My voice is silent, my vision unclear
I only have one hope in sight
That of a dim, yellow light

I wonder why things are like they are
Men being pigs, sucking cigars
Beating me up, breaking my bones
Standing over me with hearts of stone

I hear the sound of distant walking
A man's voice, quietly talking
I run for my life to get away
I try not to think of events that day

The Earth comes crashing down to my face
My pulse begins to violently race
The man approaches and darkly smiles
I won't be seeing light for a while

I try one last time to fight back
On last chance to attack
I jump up onto my numb feet
I wonder what danger I'll meet

I swing my arms in a punch
He falls to his knees with a crunch
Blood trickles down from his head
I see his face turn a dangerous red

Then I know that I can escape
Escape the world of beatings and rape
I know that I am finally free
So I run fast away, silently.

Todd Tyler (13)
Balcarras School, Cheltenham

The World We Live In

In the world we live in, there's a small lit corner
where a poor beggar lurches on a side lamp pole.
In the world we live in there's a little, old bent over man
from many years of sleeping in the roads.
In the world we live in this little, old bent over man
who lurches on a side lamp pole
he's searching in the old café bins for tonight's main course on show.
In the world we live in this dirty, mistaken soul
Is living rough through his whole life, has more knowledge that the
world's best scientists could ever produce in strife.

He watches how the world goes by, day by day
He watches as people run, shove and push
to move others from their way
he watches the expressions, happy, sad or down
he sits on the moving train line and gets a good look round.

The glares he gets from people
The abuse he receives
The sick and dirty manner of people who stare and heave.

Then a little poor farrel
A stray from home
Sits down beside him
And then begins to groan
Why does he do it?
Hit my mother so -
He say it's my fault
And how he wishes I would go.

The beggar stands up and greets him, tells him not to live this way
'I never got a chance in life, but here you must not stay

I spend my nights searching bins, trying to find the scraps of night
I sleep on cold, hard rock, when used it does not fright

So come with me now and I will find somewhere for you to go
Where a mother and a father, a family, can love you so'

So our beggar takes the poor stray to where he will be loved
And behold there is a family, the holy creature dove.

Our beggar goes back, to find a place to stand
To tell the world what life is like in this peaceful, lonely land.

Natalie O'Meara (15)
Balcarras School, Cheltenham

Generation

My generation is one of politics and power,
Could this be our final hour?
What lies around each bend?
Will the world ever end?

Is the world breaking apart?
Painting a picture, a great piece of art,
The Earth deciding the place
Of the mighty human race.

Will there ever be peace?
Where every country will feast
And there will be no wars,
No more people falling to the floor.

My generation is one of environmental threats,
How many times will there be deaths?
What is happening to our world?
Will the world be unfurled?

Mark Whistler (13)
Balcarras School, Cheltenham

My War Poem

I duck as a bullet approaches me
Soldiers fighting for their lives
One more ship arrives from sea
Guns arrive, even knives

Another friend has just gone
A bullet, that's all it takes
Just one

I wander around the trenches
Listening to the poor soldiers' retches!
The floor seems rather springy
I think it was my best mate, Zingy

War is now everywhere
And soldiers' families let fall a tear
Weapons are used in a great mass
Even terrible mustard gas

Not knowing when it will end
I say goodbye to my dying friends.

Tabitha Robinson-Wall (14)
Balcarras School, Cheltenham

Beauty

Is beauty
Only skin deep?
Is it covered up with
Make-up and searched for
In mirrors? We think we know it
When we see it, yet is real beauty in a
Face, or is it inside, unable to be seen,
Hidden by an outer shell of vanity and make-
Up, constant worry about what others think, what
They say about you behind your back, their words,
Their thoughts. Can it be seen through the cracks?
Through the mask of everyday life? Can it be
Perceived through the way we act and
Express ourselves, the colour we
Choose, the things we do?
Can we really see
Beauty? Or is
It a thing
Of the
Imagination

B
E
A
U
T
Y
.

Danni Coughlan (15)
Balcarras School, Cheltenham

Maddy's War

Her mother sat on her bed,
She closed her eyes and quietly said,
'I'm sorry darling, he's gone, he's dead.'
Late that night tears she shed.

'Don't take him, not my daddy!'
she prayed as she cried,
but it was late for little Maddy,
he had already died.

Maddy still prayed years later,
But it was no use,
She soon became a strong hater,
Of this war and abuse.

Her daddy was her hero,
He fought in World War Two,
He died for his country,
He died for me and you.

Little Maddy's still crying,
She can't deny the facts,
But she is still relying
On her daddy coming back.

Little Maddy's still crying,
She can't deny the facts,
But she is still relying
On her daddy coming back.

Little Maddy's old and frail,
Missing her daddy in his prime,
Now comes the end of this tale,
And tonight Maddy will sleep for the last time.

Chloe Mortimer-Stokes (13)
Balcarras School, Cheltenham

We Are Not Equal

Brought over in ships,
Our families, many years ago,
Beaten and struck down,
But no one heard a sound,
Owned by another,
Yet no one showed them kindness,
We are not equal.

People say it's the inside that matters,
But here outside means something too,
All men are said to be treated as equal
But the colour of our skin,
Separates us, in our world.
Water fountains, schools,
We are kept apart,
Lunch counters and buses,
We are kept apart.
We are not equal.

Those words on that sacred paper,
Jim Crow laws they're named,
Keep us apart,
We are second class citizens of America,
We are not equal.

Our non-violent protests,
Marches and sit-ins,
Freedom rides and the bus boycott,
Would these help us achieve our goals?
The black man and white man hand in hand,
Equality for all.

Frances Burton (15)
Balcarras School, Cheltenham

War

I stand, lined up with my fellow soldiers,
The man before me pulls out a gun,
The birds stop flying, the bees stop buzzing,
The gun is not brought out to stun.

He tells us to 'shoot at will,
Do not think before you kill.'
We are sent packing down to the base,
We may be followed, so run at pace.

And then the general speaks to us all,
'Good luck young soldiers, knock 'em dead for us all!'
We are sent out with great sorrow,
Will we be alive in the morrow?

The general stays put and raises a glass,
Now that's the whole lot gone, from the class.
I walk to the place where lives are lost,
We may win the war, but at what cost?

The soldiers start shooting, wanting to be the hero,
But most will probably end as another zero.
I stand quite still as an ice sculpture,
Whilst the man beside me shoots like a vulture.

Then my whole life flashes before my eyes,
My father laughs, my mother cries.
Why am I here? I don't want to die,
My eyes twitch, my mouth turns dry.

I am fighting for our land,
But I don't understand.
Why do we have to fight?
A bullet hits my heart; my life is out of sight.

James Gandhi (14)
Balcarras School, Cheltenham

Poem

His eyes open,
He grumbles as he tries to get to his feet,
His head is spinning wildly as he tries to see where he is,
He's in an alleyway,
Darkness around.

He hears a scuffle
As a rat passes him by, next to his feet,
It's cold and dingy,
And all he can think about is how he doesn't want to be this person,
Anymore.

He tramples out to the opening of the alley,
Now there is light,
People pass by and stare at him,
He's not a freak,
He has an obsession.

A shiny Bentley drives past and stops by the lights,
There is a family inside,
The children are wearing Gucci,
The parents wearing Armani.

Now it's his turn to stare.

He looks in on them like a mouse in a cage,
Thinking what it would be like to have a life like that,
If he didn't make those mistakes he did, when he was a boy,
He feels secure having a family near him, thinking it is his own,
The parents notice he's looking through the glass,
Disgust is on their faces as they pass through the green lights.

He's alone again.

If he could turn back time and say no, he would,
But they were just too quick.

They got him.

Alice Brookes (15)
Balcarras School, Cheltenham

The Iraq War

The war began and lives were lost,
Guns were fired, bombs were dropped,
Mothers crying, fathers dying,
The children only asked us 'Why?'

The war goes on and someone dies
Every day 'neath sunny skies,
Many thousand miles away,
Bad news broadcast every day.

The war on terror in 2007 started after 9/11.
We read about it everywhere,
But how many of us really care?

Long ago we fought in wars
To keep our country safe - and ours.
Our land was precious, not for the taking
Our spirit strong and not for breaking.

Now the war's a different kind,
Against evil men we cannot find,
The ones, we're told, who'll kill for fun,
The old, the young, just anyone.

We've been there now for four long years,
And all we get is death and tears,
Come home, boys, you've done your stuff,
Leave Iraq, we've had enough.

Jenny Lewis (13)
Balcarras School, Cheltenham

The Day Our Television Broke

I remember the day our television broke,
I remember feeling sad, I didn't know why the same thing was shown,
but I remember feeling sad.

A man came on our television; he mentioned death and planes,
I couldn't believe what I was hearing, the images leaving stains.
I remember seeing smoke and fumes, rise above a city,
These images weren't happy and fake, these images weren't pretty.

It was like I was watching some movie, the images sharp as a knife,
This was not a movie though, this was real life.
Why was this all happening? What had these people done wrong?
No one that day was happy; no one was all dance and song.

I remember seeing the pictures and the number of lost lives rise,
The images I was seeing, none of them were nice.
Someone was crying to the camera,
saying that they'd lost their friend,
that person's life and the victims', come to a terrible end.

The images of mass destruction were shown for days and days,
Everyone went speechless; no one knew what to say.
The television was playing the same thing now,
the images the world had viewed.
I couldn't change the pictures, the channel wasn't renewed.

I remember the day our television broke, I remember feeling sad,
I now know why the same thing was shown
and I remember feeling sad.
There had been an accident; I know exactly what,
The television told me everything, these things are not forgot.

Joe Trigg (16)
Balcarras School, Cheltenham

Where's My Spoon

Spoon.
Glorious wonder
Oh how it makes me ponder
What life is like in mine mouth
Entrance to the tunnel down south
Oh how the wondrous and liquid gold
Doth slip down my throat; like a stream
It fills the place inside, untouched by steam
Oh how I miss its heavenly silver glow
Its upside-down reflections that fill the soul
The thought of it missing harrows me still
Oh how it taunts me that it feeds another
It must be around here somewhere
It's not over there

W
H
E
R
E

I
S

M
Y

S
P
O
O
N
?

Chris Folland (15)
Balcarras School, Cheltenham

Rubbish Lot

Moonlight shines on the glass on the floor
Like an undiscovered diamond never seen before,
But the treasure's really hidden
Amongst the mess and the muck,
The scraps of food and things to sell
That you have thrown out,
Like shadows they scamper,
Up hills of pain,
That causes illness and dismay,
But choose to be there, they did not,
To live upon the rubbish lot,
To live and love and breathe and die,
There's no escape from it,
They're not dead yet,
But soon will be,
This is the price they pay to be free.

Jess Powell (15)
Balcarras School, Cheltenham

Eleven Symbols

Dreams infused by this poison fuelled night
With claret filled wounds by angered fights.
As pale, starved men stand with glowing whites,
We gazed through haze at watering eyes.

Skin soon tingled, but through the cold
Heel by heel, with a light she rolled
In one hand and in another holds
A Sunday ad, biro ink seeped into the fold.

From ale soaked skin to worn it passed
A whisper through the rim of glass
Then as she walked, scrap left behind
Eleven symbols barely seen through watering eyes.

Jake Martin (15)
Bredon School, Tewkesbury

Was It Me?

A tear fell on my cheek today,
As the newspaper told the truth,
The huge tsunami
In Miami,
Not like it used to be.

My heart thumped extra hard today,
As the news show admitted the truth,
The Shetland Islands just eroded away,
Hundreds dead,
Not like it used to be.

Was it me?
Who put a monster in the sea?

Was it me?
Who stirred up the skies and crafted the tsunami?

The world was closed today,
I was one of few alive,
But the question is
Was it me?

Emma Galton (13)
Colston's Girls' School, Bristol

Family Poem

My mum, my dad, my sister and me,
We're as happy as we can be.

My sister works through homework all night
And munches her food in tiny bites.

My mum sends my sister to bed, angrily
And I laugh at her, how she walks funnily.

My dad always makes us laugh with funny jokes,
But he laughs too much and starts to choke.

Aaghna Patel (11)
Colston's Girls' School, Bristol

My Special Place

My special place
Is where I'll go
If I'm happy or sad,
My emotions will show.

I will just stay all day,
Just thinking about things,
Forget about everything else
And hear the birds sing.

No one can disturb me,
No one knows I'm here,
It's my special place,
Out in the clear.

So this is my special place,
It's where I'll go,
Happy or sad,
My emotions can flow.

Ellie Lawrence (13)
Colston's Girls' School, Bristol

Darkness

The darkness has come and gone away,
The light is no longer welcome,
My doors are locked for evermore,
And the phone no longer rings.

The sadness inside me carries me around,
The outside noises are no longer there.
The sun has stopped shining, along with the moon and stars,
The birds no longer sing.

The life inside me has been squeezed away,
The darkness is now my friend,
There is no point to living anymore,
My world has been put to an end.

Rebecca Bailey (13)
Colston's Girls' School, Bristol

Why

You know where you are going,
to be consumed by fear and devoured by dread
to a world of merciless slaughter
to die.
To watch a sea of others do the same,
But why?

You know what you are doing,
saving your country you say,
fighting for your loved ones,
making the world a better place,
But why?

Your country's sparse of people,
your loved ones fade from crying,
awaiting your return,
knowing you are dying,
But why?

You're brave and loyal soldiers,
that is what they say,
if ever you do return
great respects to you they pay,
But why?

Do they praise you for your suffering,
Bloody wounds and rasping breath,
Because you've killed so many people,
Because you've seen so many deaths?

But why?

Savannah Sevenzo (13)
Colston's Girls' School, Bristol

Through The Eyes Of A Neglected Child

I get home from school
But my dad is out
My mum is in the kitchen
Drinking a cup of tea
Her hands are shaking
Her words a'quaking
And she is bleeding on her knee.

Is it me who caused this damage
Or is it just a curse?

My dad gets home at 8pm
He slams the door and yells
At my mum
I go running up to my den
He slams his stuff on the dining room table
Demanding some food
My mum says, 'There's none left
And don't be so rude.'

Is it me who caused this damage
Or is it just a curse?

He stands up straight
And says he's sorry
He can't stay anymore
And leaves in a hurry.

Is it me who caused the damage
Or is it just a curse?

Martha Wood (12)
Colston's Girls' School, Bristol

Girls!

Girls want this
And girls want that -
We want everything,
We're all spoilt brats!

We want the latest trends
And the coolest clothes;
We want tonnes of make-up
And powder for our nose.

But some of us are different . . .

Some want less
And some want more.
Some want that dress
But some of us are poor.
Some hate mess
And some love to bake,
Some like to mend
And some like to dance,
But some have little sisters to tend.

We all want a million pounds
To go and spend
And dine around
But now we've got our nails to mend.

We'd love to be really rich
So we could go and spend, spend, spend
But most of all
We all need a really good friend!

Katie Crowley (12)
Colston's Girls' School, Bristol

The Princess And Her Maid

Me and her
Our families are different:
They work for us
We pay them enough.

She said,
'My dad is a lawyer
My mum's an accountant
My aunty's a farmer
My family is mine.

My grandma's a seamstress
My gramps is a bookbinder
My cousin's a technician
My family is mine.

Then I said
'Well
My dad is the prince
My mum is the princess
My aunty's a duchess
My family is mine.

My grandma's a queen
My grandpa's a king
My cousin's a lord
My family is mine.

And her and me
We're both the same:
Little girls by day
Princesses by name!'

Laura Price (12)
Colston's Girls' School, Bristol

Cancer

You used to hold my hand in the park
And push me on the swings
We'd laugh at my mum in the car
When she tried to sing.

I remember your first boyfriend -
We used to double date!
But then you broke up
And we became best mates.

You always used to say you were fat,
I told you to shut up.
When I had my dance exam,
You wished me good luck.

You got some bad news;
You had cancer again,
I now know how it feels
To lose my best friend.

Ayanna Sharp (13)
Colston's Girls' School, Bristol

Pain

My mum used to say;
'Life is like a box of chocolates,'
But she's gone now.
And with that he hit me.

I miss my mum a lot.
But with a punch she was gone.
I must forget the past.
And with that he hit me.

So here I am, under my bed.
So he can't find me.
But he finds me and hits me and kicks me.
And with that I'm free.

Ocean Murphy (13)
Colston's Girls' School, Bristol

The Queen

I woke up this morning
And opened my eyes.
On the end of my bed
Sat the Queen!
I gasped and I cried,
'Gosh, when did you arrive?
Quick duck down now
Before you are seen.'

The Queen sat and laughed.
She stayed just where she was.
Said she,
'I have had quite enough,
I am going away,
You'll be Queen for the day!
You can do all the queenly stuff.'

After Queenie had left,
I wrote down some rules,
TV time ? compulsory,
By force . . .
Children won't go to school;
Grown ups have to be cool;
And your greens?
Will be banned now, of course.
Then at once I woke up
And I looked all around.
The Queen?
Nowehere to be found.
So I settled back down
And in just a few seconds,
I was asleep, quite safe
And quite sound.

Elske Waite (14)
Colston's Girls' School, Bristol

The Inconvenient Truth

Has anyone noticed the sea today?
Do they know that it's still there?
Has anyone noticed the fact that in 50 years
we will all be under water?
Has anyone noticed the sky today?
Do we even care?
Have we even noticed the ozone layer that protects us from being burnt
to a crisp?
So don't bother leaving your TV on standby,
No don't you dare, can't you see we are destroying the planet?
Yes, what you have heard is true,
in just 15 years we will all run out of gas,
'So what do we do?' I hear you say.
Recycle and protect the planet, there never was a better way.

Florence King (12)
Colston's Girls' School, Bristol

Contentment

Period of existence
In this crazy world.
Madness of conscience
Deep inside.

Deep passion inside -
Inner thoughts,
Desires,
Waiting to spring out
Like a growing flower.

Rage, when all contentment goes,
Fades into the darkness of your soul.
Lying down, not awake,
Rage takes over you.

Charlotte Rutter (14)
Colston's Girls' School, Bristol

I Miss You

I miss you so much
I miss your kindness and gentle touch
Whenever I see your favourite mug
I remember your warm, comforting hug
Whenever I daydream or think about you
I wonder - without you, what would I do?
I wait for you to come back to me
So that the happiest girl everyone can see
I wait for you to come back to me
To fly over the desert and the deep, wide sea
Sometimes I cry, but I know you don't want me to
Oh, I wish you'd come back in a day or two
I'll make my dad the greatest tea
So Daddy, please come back to me.

Reema Mobeireek (11)
Colston's Girls' School, Bristol

My Home

I wondor what it will be like in fifty years
What kind of transport will there be?
What new mobile phones will there be?
How my grandchildren will be getting on at school?
But then I stop and think about reality
That if we carry on as we are at the moment
My home will be a desert, as bare as dust
My grandchildren dead
What a world
We have no chance of surviving through the heat
All our dreams and goals poured down the sink
Everything, lost forever.

Emma Hennessey (12)
Colston's Girls' School, Bristol

Chewing Gum

I started out all wrapped up and cosy
Then fingers came in, I thought, *how nosy!*
And I was picked up, why me - not them?
Then put in a mouth, with saliva and phlegm.

I thought it disgusting, so awful - so vile!
Then I was crushed and stretched for a while.
Soon I was rudely pushed and spat out -
'Freedom. Adventure!' I loudly did shout.

But then as I flew and fell to the floor
I thought, *adventure? I want no more!*
But as I thought this, my doom descended,
When the shoe came, I thought my life had ended

So that is the reason I clung on to the shoe sole
I felt like excitement; was on a roll!
The shoe clonked up and down and around
All through this time I made not a sound.

But then the one that controlled the shoe
He noticed me and I noticed him too.
He then started scraping me with some metal thing
With a shake of his foot, me he did fling.

Here comes the irony, here comes the joke -
I landed in a bin, next to a bottle of Coke!
After some shifting, I lay for evermore
Among the rubbish, a little bit sore.

Gillian Browne (14)
Colston's Girls' School, Bristol

The Grass Grows Green

In summer the grass grows green
and sways in the gentle breeze.
Birds swoop down to steal the corn
and the air is buzzing with bees.

In autumn the grass grows short
and conkers fall to the ground.
The floor is littered with thousands of leaves
orange, yellow and brown.

In winter the grass grows muddy
and the floor is crunchy with ice.
A snowball is hurled at your window
and warm, hot chocolate tastes nice.

In spring the grass grows taller
and the flowers start to bloom.
The sun peeps out from behind a cloud
and the butterflies come out of their cocoons.

In summer the grass still grows green
but there are plans to make a new town.
A car, then a lorry, then two cranes drive past
and the trees are all chopped down.

If we don't look after our planet
there will be no more grass to grow.
Our beautiful world will be ruined by buildings
and houses in row after row.

Miranda Sadler (12)
Colston's Girls' School, Bristol

Grandpa And Me
(In memory of my grandfather Roy Purcell)

If you were ever feeling down
or even had the blues,
Grandpa was always there,
soon after his afternoon snooze.

He always used to say;
'Keep your head up and stay proud,
then you'll find your way,
through those mean, busy crowds.'

In the garden, playing catch,
while my brothers were watching the rugby match,
he always made time for me,
especially if I scraped my knee.

Smiling and laughing all the time,
singing and dancing, making up rhymes,
telling stories before bed,
just after we'd been fed.

Grandpa and me together, forever.

Since he went away,
I've been sad to this day,
I think about him every night,
from the day he took his flight.

I still feel down,
I still have the blues
I'm still laughing and smiling,
I still read before I snooze.

Together always, staying strong,
Always there, singing songs.

Grandpa and me, together forever,
Yes . . . together forever, Grandpa and me.

Jess Purcell (12)
Colston's Girls' School, Bristol

Through A Baby's Eyes

I can't talk but if I could
I'd have a lot to say.
I'd chatter on and on and on.
The whole way through the day.

But they don't know that.

I have my own opinion
And I know where stuff belongs.
I can eavesdrop on conversations,
People's natter, like gulls in song.

But they don't know that.

I have my own ways of talking,
Even if you don't understand.
It means I need the toilet,
If I wriggle and wave my hands.

But they don't know that.

I don't approve of *baby* words,
Like *choo choo train* or *doggy,*
I think they're really irritating,
Not cheerful, or funny.

But they don't know that.

Yes, I know, I'm just a baby,
Really small and really cute,
But am I not allowed to have a say?
Not allowed to contribute?
Well, let me tell you this,
I'm not as dumb as you think,
I'm actually rather clever,
But you might miss it if you blink.

But only I know that.

Emily Wright (11)
Colston's Girls' School, Bristol

Youth

Did you want to make us sin?
Do you like us to be bad?
But are we really guilty
Or is it all just mad?

Yes, some youths are guilty,
Yes, some just don't care,
But is that true for all of us,
Or do you try to scare?

Some people look at us
As if we have a gun,
Like we're taking drugs,
As if we're on the run.

Blame the media
For saying all this stuff,
About us smoking, taking drugs,
It's just a load of guff.

Charlotte Lacey (12)
Colston's Girls' School, Bristol

Ben Is Leaving

Ben is leaving.
We have two photos of him.
Our saucepan of excitement
Is bubbling with nothing but a sad little chip
Of disappointment.
Ben is leaving.
The kit list of worry is crossed off,
Yet we all know there is one item left . . .
Unwritten.
Ben is leaving.
He'd like to stay and we would too.
Why should we stop him?

Alice Stockwell (12)
Colston's Girls' School, Bristol

The Government Or Politics In My Opinion

Politics in my opinion,
(Though you may disagree),
Is in a terrible corner,
A riot, state or quandary.

The good PM for instance,
(Which tie to wear today?)
And all the press in parliament
(Who breathed a breath of late?)

And the ex-politicians,
Like John or Maggie T,
How lucky they must think themselves
To finally be free!

For though the country's run OK,
It must be a terrible place
With people running hither and thither,
I'd rather join the rat race!

Eve Miller (12)
Colston's Girls' School, Bristol

Pollution

It's this thing that sleeps,
But it drifts in our air today,
It kills the animals,
It kills the world today.

Every day we watch and play,
As the Earth is being taken away,
This is what we are causing,
As our cars are poisoning,
It is killing our world today.

Chloe Campbell (12)
Colston's Girls' School, Bristol

My Mother And Father

My mother and father love me like a piece of their own heart.
You wish you could give them something in return.

M others are the best
O pen and loving
T ake out the rubbish
H elps me with my homework
E ach morning she wakes me up
R ight early

A nd on to my dad
N ever do the clothes washing, he's
D aring and funny

F athers are caring and fab
A lthough he can be a big dummy
T all or small
H andsome or ugly
E llie still loves both her mum and dad
R eally she does.

Ellena Murphy
Colston's Girls' School, Bristol

Environment

E nergy, we're wasting it like crazy
N uclear weapons, why?
V accinations, the world needs a big one
I nfluence, it's the human influence that's killing everything
R ace, it's a race against time
O zone layer, it's got a hole in it because of us.
N ot enough fuels to last us forever
M any way to help the environment
E ven at school you can help stop pollution
N ot enough people wanting to help and understand
T reat the world with respect.

Charlotte Fletcher (13)
Colston's Girls' School, Bristol

True Love

There were two love birds
you must have heard.
They always used to say, through
rain or shine you will be mine.

They loved so much, you'd never guess
they even passed the lover's test.
They always used to say, through
rain or shine you will be mine.

They went through fun times, they went through rough,
but they still didn't get enough.
They always used to say, through
rain or shine you will be mine.

They loved so much, it would break your heart,
but suddenly they were torn apart.
But they still said, through
rain or shine you will be mine.

Now they live in hatred and pain,
will they ever see each other again?
They used to say, through
rain or shine you will be mine.

But years had passed, days had flown,
so she decided to ring his telephone.
They always used to say, through
rain or shine you will be mine.

He heard the ringing in his head,
he picked it up and then he said,
Through rain or shine
you will be mine.

Frances Murphy (11)
Colston's Girls' School, Bristol

Raindrops

As I look across the colourful field,
Thinking how beautiful it is,
How man could build flats or multi-storey car parks
On such a wonderful place, I will never know.

I look over at the wood,
People cut down forests every day,
These are keeping us alive,
Look after it, or it will stop.

I look at the stream,
Remembering the polluted waters in the canal,
Water we need to drink,
But it's now to unsafe to even touch.

I look at the fields,
Wildflowers, bracken and poppies blowing in the breeze,
The real world where we belong,
Is nearly far behind,
Bring it back and start again.

We're all raindrops,
Individually tiny, but when working together
We can make a difference.

Kimberley Jones (13)
Colston's Girls' School, Bristol

The Photo Album

I sat and looked at the photos,
Of when me and her were young
And remembering all those memories
Of when we had so much fun.

Like lightning without thunder,
Without fishes in the sea,
Like day without sunlight,
Without her and me.

But she was three years older
And she had loads of mates,
Dolls got replaced with make-up,
Slamming doors and smashing plates.

Her temper was so much worse,
Until the memories were on the haze,
Playing cops and robbers,
Were the good old days.

I don't think she notices,
My sister's the missing part,
And on a whim, just maybe,
She has space for me in her heart.

Evleen Price (12)
Colston's Girls' School, Bristol

The Cats Go Splat

Once there were two evil cats,
And their names were Frank and Bill.
Instead of just chasing rats,
They'd rather eat without a kill.

These two cats, they once did steal
Two hamburgers for their evening meal.
Instead of just chasing rats,
They'd rather eat without a kill.

They did find a toffee pudding
And they did not feel too ill.
Instead of just chasing rats,
They'd rather eat without a kill.

So they tried to pounce on it,
Pounce onto the window sill,
Instead of just chasing rats,
They'd rather eat without a kill.

Once it was in their mouths,
It tasted like Uncle Bill.
Instead of just chasing rats,
They'd rather eat without a kill.

They did choke and just faint
Into the kitchen grill.
Instead of just chasing rats,
They'd rather eat without a kill.

Alexandra Denny (11)
Colston's Girls' School, Bristol

It's Your Fault

It's an inconvenient truth you know,
The fact that I'm always here to stay,
I did not want to have to come,
But you insisted on me staying to play,
You begged you cried and did so many things,
What you've put me through is terrible.

You used all my clients,
Cars, aeroplanes, litter,
Just so you could get to me,
And now I feel bitter.

I eat up all of your values,
Just like a compost bin,
I make people ill,
Give a funny smell,
I'll make you life a misery,
It's just part of me.

There are many ways for me to go,
You just cannot see,
Your so called future, you don't care about,
Happens to rely on me,
Recycle, reuse, repay,
The world we live in,
I've had my time, let me go,
It's up to you, it's your life you know.

Mariam Olatidoye (12)
Colston's Girls' School, Bristol

The Burning Sea

A fire on the hilltops,
Burning like the sun.
Flames growing every second,
Rising one by one.

The sea is rippling beneath it,
Blue it used to be.
Now it reflects orange,
We call it the burning sea.

The trees burning, like charcoal,
Black as the dead night.
Birds that were nesting way up high,
Have lost all sense of flight.

The sky is being polluted,
Smoke is all you see.
Orange glimmers down below,
We call it the burning sea.

Katie Smith (12)
Colston's Girls' School, Bristol

Darkness

Darkness everywhere
That's what it's always been.
No colours of the rainbow,
No love at first sight,
No emotions to be seen.
That's the way it's always been.
Not to see things
Might seem strange to you,
But not to me,
'Cause that's the way it's always been.

Sophia Doughty (12)
Colston's Girls' School, Bristol

Pollution

Pollution is all around us,
It is poisoning the world,
Even though we can't see it,
It's getting worse and worse.

Pollution is all around us,
Black smoke everywhere,
Making us crack down,
On what we buy to share.

Pollution is all around us,
Making us feel guilty,
Pollution is all around us,
To make us stop and think.

Pollution is all around us,
It never goes away,
Pollution is all around us,
It will always stay.

Hannah Cullum (12)
Colston's Girls' School, Bristol

Love

Love is pink
Like a pink loveheart.
It feels like you're ready
To pump out happiness!
Love looks like people wanting to kiss
It sounds like the beat of a heart.
It reminds me of my parents,
In the sunshine of Portugal.
The most happy I've ever been!

Lois Linter (12)
Colston's Girls' School, Bristol

Environment

One day, one day
I hope and pray that the threat of global warming will stop casting
the long shadow of doom over us all,
One day, one day
I hope and pray the one day the oil companies will comprehend the
nature of the tragic disaster that they are creating,
so pollution won't roam the skies.

I wish, I wish
That we did not cause any threat to those animals
that were affected by our actions,
I wish, I wish
We did not act so cowardly and turn the opposite way,
saying it's only one car, it's only one factory,
when it's much more than that.

Global warming isn't hard to explain,
It leaves Mother Nature crying with excruciating pain.
We need to stop it now so the temperature doesn't rise.
People, plants and animals would be in demise.
Burning hot temperatures, more gases in our air,
Overloading Mother Nature; does anyone really care?

Alisha Litt (12)
Colston's Girls' School, Bristol

It's Our Choice

I am here,
I am there,
I am everywhere!

I am in the air and I am scattered across the ground.
I cause many problems to you, I spread misery onto your paths,
but clearly you don't mind, as you are the ones who create me!

You scatter me around on the ground, you give me life.
I thank you ever so much for that.
But don't mind me saying,
Don't you care?

Don't you want to live in a clean and tidy environment?
Instead of having me to pollute and cause havoc to your environment.
Well, at the end of the day
It is your choice.
I'm just making a suggestion.

Anmol Anjam (12)
Colston's Girls' School, Bristol

The Environment

The cars race down the motorway,
Rushing, rushing,
Smoke billowing from the exhaust like an old man's pipe;
Burning, burning,
Through our world, the Earth.

As technology rises, with many more factories,
Working, working,
Polluting the atmosphere,
Burning, burning,
Through our world, the Earth.

Our world is slowly heating up,
Heating, heating,
What can we do to stop it?
Burning, burning,
Nothing will be left, like a burnt out pipe.

Lydia Barnes (12)
Colston's Girls' School, Bristol

The Window

I sit down, look out the window
and I watch,
I watch people slowly and
unknowingly destroy the world.
People in houses watching TV
and playing on computers.
I think, why does no one care?
Is anyone in the know?
If no one acts fast the world
will be no more.

People are told at last and still no one
seems to care.
We are all too lazy and are way too
comfortable to act on it.

At last I see someone put up
solar panels, but that is just
one in a million.
Still hundreds to go.

Mattie Ward (13)
Colston's Girls' School, Bristol

Is This The World Today

Gosh, goodness me,
I can't believe people now.
They go around shouting out,
'You're a bitch! She's a cow!'

At 11 o'clock at night,
Coming home from a play,
Men jump on the car
And say, 'Oh man, you're so gay!'

Women with their ways,
Heels and mini skirts.
The middle of winter
And they're wearing tiny shirts.

I tell you that the world
Is turning rather weird.
High streets are in chaos,
It's exactly what I feared.

I don't feel safe now,
Walking home at night.
The danger someone'll jump out,
The threat they'll start a fight.

I'd try to hit them back,
But they'd be stronger than me.
That is what I think about,
That is what I see.

These days I rarely go out,
Now I'm getting old.
People seem so scary,
I no longer feel so bold.

Kate Brennan (12)
Colston's Girls' School, Bristol

What Is Life?

Life is a journey, a long way to go,
At times it is fast, at times it is slow,
The road can be bumpy with trouble and tears,
But friendship and love can end all our fears.

Life's an adventure, there's so much to see,
From fish in the ocean to birds in the trees,
The road can be bumpy with trouble and tears,
But friendship and love can end all our fears.

Life can be painful when people are cruel,
Children are starving while others have jewels,
The road can be bumpy with trouble and tears,
But friendship and love can end all our fears.

Without friendship and someone to trust,
Life can be lonely and very unjust,
The road can be bumpy with trouble and tears,
But friendship and love can end all our fears.

Life brings its worries, doubts and fears,
Although people listen they don't always hear,
The road can be bumpy with trouble and tears,
But friendship and love can end all our fears.

Give happiness to others, you'll be amazed,
At how it can help in so many ways,
The road can be bumpy with trouble and tears,
But friendship and love can end all our fears.

My life is amazing, I love being me,
I can't wait to discover what I will be,
The road can be bumpy with trouble and tears,
But friendship and love can end all our fears.

Anna Lawrence (11)
Colston's Girls' School, Bristol

Up

Stand up now, show us you can,
It will always be fine.

Up, up, up,
Going up forever.
Always there, reaching,
Reaching for our life.

Just hold yourself up,
Up through the mist,
Up through the cloud,
Into your own safe place.

We are the world,
Spinning because of life,
Twisting down into our hollow cradles,
Twirling, falling, laughing.

I want to be me,
Not you,
Not a leaf,
Just me.

It will always be fine,
Even when you are a leaf,
Blown by the wind,
Tumbling gracefully down.

Pointing upwards,
Frolicking and giggling,
Falling and laughing,
Keeping on forever.

Just get up, get up now,
Keep yourself reaching,
Always keep on reaching,
Reaching for the light.

Rose Juliet (12)
Colston's Girls' School, Bristol

My Faith

The church,
Not a steeple,
Not a building,
But linked in the Holy Spirit,
It's the people.

My faith holds on,
My faith carries on.

No dairy, no wheat,
My healing
Made me free,
I was held in chains,
But now I can be me.

My faith holds on,
My faith carries on.

He's alive,
He rose from the dead,
Dying for our sins,
He died for me
And didn't run when He could have fled.

My faith holds on,
My faith carries on.

Freedom,
That's what He can give.
Admit your sin,
Say you were wrong
And you He will forgive.

My faith can be yours,
If you believe.
Our faith holds on,
Our faith carries on.

Ruth Walker
Colston's Girls' School, Bristol

Petnapper Problem

There were two puppies, left all on their own,
The family went on holiday and left them a bone.
They wandered the street, looking to play,
But all they found was death and decay.

Over the fence and gate they jumped,
Looking for something that was pumped.
They wandered the street, looking to play,
But all they found was death and decay.

The rugby match was on that day,
So nobody did come out to play.
They wandered the street, looking to play,
But all they found was death and decay.

All they saw was a drunken man,
Sitting alone sipping coffee in a van.
They wandered the street, looking to play,
But all they found was death and decay.

The pups went up and sniffed the van,
When unexpectedly, out popped the man.
They wandered the street, looking to play,
But all they found was death and decay.

He snatched them up and put them in
The front of the van, along with him.
They wandered the street, looking to play,
But all they found was death and decay.

The next day when the family came back,
The puppies were not out the back.
They wandered the street, looking to play,
But all they found was death and decay.

Isabelle Craner (11)
Colston's Girls' School, Bristol

Wonderful

An avenue of maple covered net,
we are still to watch the sun set.
Wonderful world, you blessed my heart,
Wonderful world when did it start?

There's a carriage waiting at the bottom of the street,
you just name the time and there we'll meet.
Wonderful world, you blessed my heart,
Wonderful world when did it start?

A glowing light is coming from afar,
as you wish on a shooting star.
Wonderful world, you blessed my heart,
Wonderful world when did it start?

Silky snow, you give affection,
water so clear there's all reflection.
Wonderful world, you blessed my heart,
Wonderful world when did it start?

There's a young polar bear, he wishes only to learn
and if he takes it step by step soon will come his turn.
Wonderful world, you blessed my heart,
Wonderful world when did it start?

The beautiful places you left us, which we can all help preserve,
but should we really take the things that we don't deserve?
Wonderful world, you blessed my heart,
Wonderful world when did it start?

Will you stay, oh Lord, forever
or will you go away and never?
Wonderful world, you blessed my heart,
Wonderful world when did it start?

Daisy Miller (11)
Colston's Girls' School, Bristol

A Tale Of Gold

You hear about pirates, sailing the sea,
who sailed day by day on the breeze,
so now the story will be told,
about how pirates stole for gold.

We looked at islands, secret caves,
we lived in a time of wizards and knaves,
so now the story will be told,
about how pirates stole for gold.

On one adventurous, dangerous trip,
a man called Jack gave us the slip,
so now the story will be told,
about how pirates stole for gold.

We went into a cave so dark and black,
then the man made a very loud crack!
so now the story will be told,
about how pirates stole for gold.

The cave fell in, no one survived,
now we can't live life on the tide,
so now the story will be told,
about how pirates stole for gold.

Now we are buried in rubble, we cry,
we are not ready to say our goodbyes,
so now the story has been told,
about how we tried to steal gold.

Ayla Norman (11)
Colston's Girls' School, Bristol

My Aunty

Will she die? I asked.

We are sitting on a bus,
My mum has just told me that my aunty is ill.

I stare out of the window,
I feel like the world is crashing down around me,
I am scared.
Will I ever see her again?
I try to hold it in, but my emotions are too strong.

I cry,
What am I going to do?
Sit and sob, or
Face up to it?
I miss her,
I want to be by her side,
There is something I want to say to her first,
I love you.

Meg Lawrence (12)
Colston's Girls' School, Bristol

Hero Of The Day

If I had to pick,
A hero of the day,
Today it would be my nan,
Because she's a hero in every way.

No matter what she's faced with,
She's strong throughout it all,
With friends and family around her,
Big, small and tall.

And that is why she is my hero.

My hero of the day.

Amy Hillier (12)
Downend School, Bristol

Never Again

We were taken by a nice man, well, my parents thought so anyway,
But once my home was out of sight, he became sinister,
All of my brothers perished and were dumped.

Never again will I sit in the dark,
Bruises all over.
Tired, weak girls fumble in the darkness,
We were together but alone.

The van stopped.
My sister and I were marched into a dingy, dark room,
We were chained to the wall.
One girl didn't get many customers, she was taken away.

Never again will I sit in the dark,
Bruises all over.
Tired, weak girls fumble in the darkness,
We were together but alone.

As soon as someone disappeared,
Another, thin, melancholy girl took her place. Food was scarce,
In the rare event of any,
Those who dared ask for more were beaten.

Never again will I sit in the dark,
Bruises all over.
Tired, weak girls fumble in the darkness,
We were together but alone.

Customers jeered and did what they liked with us,
They forced us to have sex, then they left.
Our captor received paper notes
like the ones my parents gave him long ago.

A kindly face reveals a way out,
Walk away, run away, now I am free!

I drift with the wind, my life has purpose, my childhood is past me.
Never again, never again, never again.

Katriona Pierce (12)
Hayesfield School, Bath

Talkin' 'Bout Our Generation

Talkin' 'bout our generation
What goes through your mind,
When you see a few teenagers in the street?

Do you anxiously move around them on the other side of the road?
Turn around, walk in the opposite direction?

Thoughts flash through your head
Thinking about your days of childhood
Saying, 'What did I used to do?'
Or maybe, ahead
Thinking, 'What will I be doing?'

Washing for the family?
'Twas a long time ago
Or maybe sleeping in late
Staying out at night
Making your mark at school?

Maybe they're not so bad
Lounging in the streets
Scaring you away.

Olivia De Miceli (12)
Hayesfield School, Bath

The Sun

My light beams out,
all day, all the while
to light my home and spread my smile.
Until the moon rises from the deep
and tucks me in to my deep sleep.

I sleep at night,
to save my energy,
to save my light,
so I can shine the city white.

Bethany Stenning (12)
Hayesfield School, Bath

Why

It's dark
Not night-time dark, just black.
It's always been dark for me,
There is nothing before my eyes,
Never has been, never will be.

People try to describe my surroundings,
All the while I'm craving, craving to see it too,
To enjoy the privileges everyone takes for granted.

Maybe, just maybe though,
Everyone sees things differently.
Maybe her pink is his brown,
Maybe all of us see the world in our own way
And some can't see it all.

And why, anyway?
Why are we here?
Why are some deaf, some blind?
Why does the door of life shut as quickly as it was opened?
Or is life some big mistake? A dream?
Will we wake up in some other place
And laugh at a weird dream
About life in a fantasy place called Earth?

Why is it me?
It's black,
Why?
I can't see like you.
Why?

Bryony Parsons (12)
Hayesfield School, Bath

Titanic

As this ship is sinking,
I write this letter,
Hopeful someone should find it,
In a thousand years to come.

Where is my love?
Where could he be?
Is this the end of me?
What should I do?

Why does this happen to me?
What have I done?
Is it a dream
Or is it reality?

This is the end of my journey
As the ship goes down.
I had a good life,
So this is goodbye.

Melissa Pope (13)
Hayesfield School, Bath

Space

Zoom, in the spaceship,
flying past the shining stars,
I think it's time for a little kip,
wait a sec, it's Mars!
I think I'll have to stay awake,
there seems to be big boulders passing,
but then again I'll have some cake,
all the crew seem to be gassing,
we're going back to Earth, one spoke,
so we turned around and headed back.
'That's not fair,' I said, as I nearly choked,
now we must all pack!

Tillie Jarvis (12)
Hayesfield School, Bath

What Do You Think

I look out of the window.
What do I see?
Three buzzing bees
And a honeysuckle tree.

How did they get here?
How come we can see?
How was the planet created?
One, two, three . . .

Mercury, Venus,
Earth and Mars,
The moon, sun
And wonderful stars!

Each living person
Has a mind of their own,
Comfort and warmth
In their precious home.

Family and friends,
Food and drink,
All these things we could not live without.
What do you think?

Jessica Clothier (12)
Hayesfield School, Bath

Our Planet

Raindrops, pouring in the summer
Leaves falling in spring
Heatwave in the winter
Now what will autumn bring

This seasonal weather change
Is how it should be in Australia
Our attempt to save the world
Has been an utter failure

The polar caps are melting
So if we don't do something soon
The world will overflow
And we'll evacuate to the moon

So do your bit for the world
Recycle loads and loads
Remember to turn off the lights
Make less use of the roads

And if we all do this together
The outcome will be bold
Then up there where the penguins live
It might actually be cold!

Ellie Frank (12)
Hayesfield School, Bath

Listen

I remember my first day at school,
I could hear things but not speak,
I know the answer, I'm no fool,
No one thinks to ask.

I went to the doctors, to get checked out,
But I could not get the message across,
What if it's cancer, I thought to myself,
He had no time to find out.

When I tripped and banged my head,
I couldn't call for help.
No one can hear a silent scream,
If it weren't for that boy, I might be dead.

I wanted to be in the Navy,
To hold my head up high,
I couldn't shout commands though,
So my lifelong dream was lost.

I've spent my life alone now,
Drivers shouting, children laughing,
No one to comfort me, but it's made me strong,
Ready to fight, fight to say, 'It's not right.'

Emily Appleby-Matthews (12)
Hayesfield School, Bath

Lost At Sea

Drifting in my sail boat, no one else in sight,
I find myself alone with blue all around.
I try to find some land, but there isn't land in sight,
There are small, beautiful fishes, swimming, everywhere I look.
Where am I?
Where can I be?
I am in the middle of the sea,
Lost at sea.

Amber Harrup (12)
Hayesfield School, Bath

Evie The Cat

My name is Evie, I am a cat.
Why do you stare at my features like that?
Haven't you noticed my shape is divine?
And that's mentioning my silvery sheen!
Tell me, why do stare like that?
Do you mistake my curves for blubbery fat?
Haven't you noticed the tom-cats love me?
I'm sure it helps that I'm soft and fluffy.
Really, what's up, with that awful glare?
Desist now with your sickening stare!
You may tell me my eyes look like snot,
But let me tell you, an oil painting you're not.
You may not like how I act,
You may not like how I look,
But one thing is for sure -
My confidence will not be shook!

Sophie Gwilt (12)
Hayesfield School, Bath

No One Knows

No one knows how I feel,
I am like a robot - I speak with an electronic voice.
I have forgotten the taste of food - I am fed by a tube.
I survive on liquids, nothing else.
I always feel angry and upset.
I can't run it off, I'm stuck in my wheelchair.
My life seems small and narrow,
Like an endless dark passage,
With no way out.
Why did my brain grow a tumour?
Why can't I be like I was before?
No one knows.

Alissa Tooley (12)
Hayesfield School, Bath

Homeless

Dark doorway,
Feeling cold,
No one to love me,
No one to hold.
Belly rumbling,
Nothing to eat,
No one to talk to,
Tired, aching feet.

Sat on the floor,
Day after day,
Feeling like no one,
Nothing to say.
Children laughing,
Being ignored,
Hour after hour
Of feeling bored.

Each hour is the same,
Angry and sad,
Feeling so worthless,
Am I so bad?
The tramp of feet,
Not catching my eye,
Time dragging on,
Waiting to die.

Isabel Williams (12)
Hayesfield School, Bath

Look At Me

Look at me,
I'm sitting here in shabby clothes,
Shaking my tin, hearing nothing from within,
I'm homeless.

Look at me,
The nights are drawing in, what can I do?
Wrap up tight, hoping the moon stays bright,
I'm homeless.

Look at me,
Living all alone,
Sitting on a shop corner, wishing it were warmer,
I'm homeless.

Hey over here,
I smell,
I'm cold,
I cry.

I'm alone,
Growing old,
Help me,
I'm homeless.

Look at me,
Told to go away,
Dusting myself down, while I turn around,
Walking the other way.

Charlotte Imianowski (13)
Hayesfield School, Bath

Frog

I like you Frog,
When I hold you in my hand
I can feel you breathing.

I notice the green-brown of your skin,
Your golden flecks, your eyes like glass beads,
I feel your bones, fragile like a bird's.

The surprising softness of your belly,
Your legs are stretched like a ballet dancer's.
Your skin is not slimy but cool and could tear easily.

You live in my grandmother's pond, under the rocks and the weeds.
Sometimes we find tiny frogs' skeletons
behind the Aga in the kitchen,
Hunched up, intricate and tangled in cobwebs.

Where do you go in winter?
When I'm warm in my bed, you're still out there,
In the black waters of the pond.

There's something foreign about you, Frog.
Uncomplaining, solitary, alone.
I like you.

Sashia Webb-Hayward (12)
Hayesfield School, Bath

Silver Love

A burst of lightning, a rumble of thunder in the distance
A shadow illuminated against a silver moon.
The night is cloaked in a mantle of shadows
And the stars glisten in the night

Loneliness presses down on me as I lie on the ground
The sky above seems so close tonight
The night where my heart has left me
And left a gaping hole in my soul

I was in love with a boy
Blue-eyed angel with blond locks
But one problem
How can you love but it is not returned?

Oh how I wish that love had
Not taken me in its arms
And twisted my heart to
Hate and love

A fragrant flower blooms beside me
A small, silver flower, with dewdrops hanging down
It refreshes my and my heart begins to beat
Hope heals my soul.

Lauren Schofield (13)
Hayesfield School, Bath

My Biggest Dream

I want something so much
but it costs such a lot
it's my biggest dream come true
what can I do?

I think about it all the time
will it come true?
It's selfish of me to ask
when it costs more than you.

I ask my mum
She says, 'Maybe, one day'
Or is that just what they say?

Sometimes I think I'm there
I know it's just a dream
I know it isn't reality
It's just another daydream.

Will it become reality?
It's everything I need.
I know it's just a country,
but it's my biggest dream.

Bethany Mitchell (13)
Hayesfield School, Bath

Passing By

Who am I?
A sister, a father, a mother, a brother?
An orphan, with no one to turn to?
Did you really see me at all?
I'll tell you,
I'm the stranger passing by,
A strand of memory slipping down the drain,
Never saying hello or goodbye,
You'll never know me like a friend.

I'm just a stranger passing by.

I have friends, I have enemies,
I'm a shadow on a wall,
A flash in the corner of your eye.

I'm just a stranger passing by.

I'm that guy in the supermarket,
That girl on the bus,
The friend you lost when you were young.

I'm just a stranger passing by.

Bethany Davison (12)
Hayesfield School, Bath

Christmas Eve

Fire blazes in the hearth,
Banishing the winter chill,
A fresh mince pie, that's warm and waiting,
Sits upon the window sill.

Fairylights that gleam and sparkle,
Seven stockings in a row.
All is silent, all are sleeping,
As, at last, it starts to snow.

The sound of bells rings through the heavens,
Dancing into children's dreams.
The moon rides high upon the sky,
As in its light the fresh snow gleams.

In the morning, children waking,
Children crying out with joy,
Opening mysterious parcels,
One for every girl and boy.

Chloë Meanwell (12)
Hayesfield School, Bath

Just Try To Wonder

Is it ever wondered,
What is the meaning of this?
The sheer, downright beauty,
The everlasting bliss.

Is it ever wondered
How the air we breathe came to be?
How the birds fly through it,
The creation of waves in the sea?

Is it ever wondered,
If we were meant to be here?
Why were we placed in this haven?
Someone make it clear.

Megan Hazell (13)
Hayesfield School, Bath

Fields Of Clover

As I wander through fields of lush emerald grass and clover,
I am happy.
My legs are surrounded by dancing leaves,
Singing and rustling through the air.
A symphony of sounds.
A soft breeze flows through my hair,
It ripples through the trees
And creates the image of a green sea.
Flowers everywhere bring forth melodies,
But not those you can hear.
It is a visible melody,
A melody of colours.
Bright daffodils and buttercups,
Yellow as the sun,
Grow amongst poppies, red as a sunset.
The azure sky reflects all this beauty,
Together with the hills,
Rolling gently to the distant horizon.

Imogen Ely (12)
Hayesfield School, Bath

Alone In The Playground

He stands there, in the middle of the playground,
His arms swinging from left to right,
As the wind blows wildly.
He stands there, all alone and cold,
Waiting for summer to come
And his leaves to come back.
Weeks pass and the weather's getting warmer,
When one Monday morning he is awoken
By the sound of schoolchildren playing.
Standing in the middle of the playground,
He is no longer alone.

Kirsty Smith (13)
Hayesfield School, Bath

I Saw You

I saw you,
Lying there,
Helpless,
Anxious.

Then I saw him,
Sitting there,
Scared,
Lonely.

I felt awful!
What could I do?
How could I help you
When I was scared myself?

So, I just sat there,
Staring,
Intrigued, but heartbroken.

When did our society fall apart?
How has it sunk this low?
How could they let you get like this?

Then I left,
I abandoned you,
How could I?
I just went.

Weeks later, I turned on the TV,
Saw the news,
And there you were, lying there,
Unconscious,
Abandoned.
Dead.

Bethany Walls (12)
Hayesfield School, Bath

Changing the World . . .

One day I woke up
and here's what I thought I'd do, if I could change the world for good.
How much better would this Earth be, if I could?

There'd be no pointless wars,
there'd be no poverty,
there'd be no threat of global warming,
Oh, how much better the world would be!

There wouldn't be any murders,
there wouldn't be any bullies,
there wouldn't be any bad crimes committed,
Oh, make this so, please!

There would be no fighting,
no bad political stuff,
there would be no one left out in the cold,
and everyone would be friends, yes, I think that's enough.

One day I woke up
and that's what I thought I'd do,
if I were to change the world for good.
Tell me you don't wish the same,
I know that all of you would.

Maddie Dawes (13)
Hayesfield School, Bath

If . . .

What if the world was plagued with darkness
Everyone invisible, no eyes could see
Nothing would sparkle, nothing would glitter
Except for the love between you and me
I wouldn't see you, but would feel your touch
And smell your warm, sweet scent.

Alice Ware (13)
Hayesfield School, Bath

Our Generation

He lays there, in his bed asleep,
Dreaming small and magical things.
He lays there, watching the moon
As it peers through the curtain
Telling its tales.

In the year 2007,
Gun crime is at a high,
As many die, we say goodbye.
Carbon emissions damage the world,
Governments start building on fields.

His eyes start to close
As he starts to doze,
The moon continues its tales.

Chelsea Buchan (13)
Hayesfield School, Bath

Generation Gap

Conversations with my grandad
Are like school time sessions!
He always says, 'You're the teacher, lass!'
It's like modern language lessons!

And when I'm talkin' 'bout my school,
Grandad rambles on . . .
'We didn't have a fancy pool,
or a gymnasium.'

Sometimes grandad doesn't understand me,
and I don't understand him,
he's constantly losing his front door key,
I think it's an ageing thing!

Emma Park (12)
Hayesfield School, Bath

Through The Eyes Of . . .

The stars shine, chilly, in the sky,
Jumping from roof to roof, I can almost fly,
The heart that doesn't beat beneath my chest,
Frozen, eternally without rest.
My coat is wrapped around me like the night,
With my gun in hand I take flight,
As I land upon the ground,
Careful not to make a sound,
You turn around to face me,
I half expect you to flee,
But the look of shock upon your face,
I wish would vanish without a trace.
I advance towards you, standing there,
Convincing myself I do not care
That your life is coming to an end,
To hell I will send
Your immortal soul.
Your suffering in my hands I hold,
I put the gun up to your head
And pull the trigger. *Bang!* you're dead!
Your corpse is sprawled upon the ground,
You will lie there until you're found,
My razor-sharp white teeth, rip out your throat,
Damning you to a tortuous fate.

Lily Jennings (13)
Hayesfield School, Bath

Dumped

Lost in the dark
Lonely and cold
Nowhere to hide
No one to hold
Nowhere to run
Nothing to see
It's just me

I was dumped
I was whacked
I was bumped
I was smacked
Bruised and hurt
They left me

I'm just a puppy
Why do I deserve this?

Lost in sorrow
Overcome with joy
I can't believe it
They have found me!

Lucy Boan (10)
Hayesfield School, Bath

Fame Too Soon . . .

'Isn't she lucky, that Hollywood girl?

She had everything she wanted
From diamonds to pearls.'
These words were spoken by a girl who had it all too soon.
But then her life fell apart
Like a crumbling dune.

They took it from her
Those diamonds and pearls
And sooner than thought
Survival was her world.

Pushing herself to climb to the top
This girl searching for fame
She just cannot stop.

Losing everything
Her family, her friends.
Who'll ever know
When this escapade will end.

Sedona Ferguson (13)
Hayesfield School, Bath

Exit The Old, Enter The New

These day you can't . . .
Build a go-kart with ease, courtesy of the bad prams
Build a tree house, all thanks to health and safety
Go fishing - all the rivers you cannot linger in.

Instead it's all . . .
3rd generation consoles, fighting for control of the market
Over-expensive handhelds,
People staying up half the night, just for the latest book or game.

Companies and minors,
taking each other to court for the most pathetic reasons.

New cars coming out
No longer the powerful horsepower hungry beasts
that they once were.
It's now all about the environment, efficiency, comfort.
There were once machines of beauty.
Now it's all carbon fibre curves and inverted two-toned paint.

My generation, full of anti-social louts.

Tom Hawkins (12)
Minehead Middle School, Minehead

My Generation

My generation
Is an inspiration
To the nation

Our generation makes mistakes
But we rise to high stakes
We know what it takes
To stop this disgrace
Of war and global warming

If we try now
This trouble will be over
And this whole thing will be a memory.

Rayne Holland-Smith (12)
Minehead Middle School, Minehead

Talkin' 'Bout My Generation

Autumn, children in the leaves, playing around
Fires are on in houses to keep us warm
Children wrapped up warm
Leaves falling down on us

Hallowe'en, children knocking on the doors
Scaring people and getting sweets
Walking with their parents and older brother and sister
Then going home to eat the sweets

Christmas, children waiting till the morning
Father Christmas delivering presents to us
Snow is falling, getting deep
People going to sleep

Birthday, children opening presents
Getting ready for school to see their friends
After school going home to get ready for party
Party going on, blowing candles out and giving out cake.

Alysha Kendall (12)
Minehead Middle School, Minehead

My Generation

Bikes are sweet
I like to sit on my seat
I go mountain biking
And my parents don't like hiking
Mountain biking is cool
I like swimming in the swimming pool
We haven't got much room
But we still go up to the Combe
In this school we do a lot of petitions
That's why I should win the competition.

Dan Farmer (12)
Minehead Middle School, Minehead

Stop Horse Slaughter

Scared, worried and frightened
Upset, afraid and petrified
I am bundled into a trailer
With no hope to survive.

I finally arrive, after hours of exhaustion
I am unloaded by vicious men
Suddenly I hear lots of banging
And horses neighing.

They are telling me to run
Run for my life
But it's too late
I'm being taken into a dark room

I see my best friend go in front
They take a knife
And they stab him
Twice

He neighs to me, saying goodbye
Why?
He hasn't done anything wrong
Then I realise it's me next

They shoot me in the head
It bangs around my body
Then
I drop dead.

Elsie Berry (12)
Minehead Middle School, Minehead

Changes

The hill over there
Has been there for some years
Not touched not moved
Just stays there and lingers

Five years later
It'll still be there
Not touched, not moved
Just stays there and lingers

It stands there
All on its own
With absolutely
Nothing at all

But people do not notice
The things that do not change
They look, they stare
Then go away again

Then one day
They will come back
Maybe have a picnic
Maybe go on a hack

I'd be surprised if people noticed
The hill over there
Not touched, not moved
Just stays there and lingers.

Francesca Broome (11)
Minehead Middle School, Minehead

Kitty Kat

I love my cats, I really do,
Sometimes I think they belong in a zoo.
When they were born, they were really small,
But now they've grown so shockingly tall.

They play around and growl at each other,
They go outside and scowl at another.
They scratch and bite, then lick you instead
And then you just have to pat them on the head.

Scared of dogs, like chewing logs,
Following people on their daily jogs.
Miaowing like mad, looking sad,
When really most of the time they're glad.

Call their names, hear them run,
Running until they reach the sun.
Then they come in and sit on a mat,
This poem's about my Kitty Cat.

Gabriella Routley (12)
Minehead Middle School, Minehead

My Poem

M y generation is full of cool stuff
Y es, the world's high-tech

G ordon Brown runs the country
E ven though no one likes him
N ever mind, he's better than Blair
E ggheads give us lots of answers
R ugby teams are all rubbish
A ll except the mighty England
T o the final we go
I nto the Stade de France
O wning South Africa
N ot the other way round.

Callum Langley (12)
Minehead Middle School, Minehead

Who Is He?

He is a man
A real gentleman
Kind to me in every way
Never looks at me without a smile

Different from other boys
Special
Warming my heart
Every minute of every hour

He is like a ball of cotton to a cat
One in a million
Unique in his own way
Always there for me

He is my boyfriend
Algene
8 months it's been now
Happy as ever!

Jessie Evans (12)
Minehead Middle School, Minehead

Global Warming

Global warming's effect

The wildlife is beautiful,
We need to be careful.

'Cause global warming is going to start,
We need all scientists to be smart.

In places the water is going to rise,
Causing a very big surprise.

All people need to think,
About younger people, so they don't sink.

Viki Jones (12)
Minehead Middle School, Minehead

The World Is Moving On

Technology these days
Has grown quite a lot,
I wish I could have seen it,
When is was first a plant pot

When you have the right space,
You know what to do,
Let the roots grow big and strong,
Oh look, your email's coming through

First there's PCs,
Then there is chat,
Next there will be robots,
Even holographic hats

Let this tree keep growing,
Water it every day,
It will have its memories
When it passes away

Technology now,
Is getting once more
Still wish I could have seen it
When it was first born.

Jonathan Leary-Hemans (12)
Minehead Middle School, Minehead

My Broken Leg

I cleared the jump the first time
Then I tried again
It went wrong the second time
I ended up in pain.

I screamed so loud it hurt my throat
My friend he had to phone.
My mum arrived in record time
She couldn't take me home.

The doctor said I'd broken it
It was really bad.
They put it in loads of plaster
I was really sad.
They pushed me in a wheelchair,
I missed loads of school.
Why had I been so stupid?
Life can be really cruel.

Six weeks passed so slowly
I couldn't wait to be
Out of this plaster of Paris
And to have my leg free.

Daniel Thompson (12)
Minehead Middle School, Minehead

Cricket

Beefy
Blackwell
Durston
My heroes, all of them
But one thing joins the three
They are all in cricket history
All three played for Somerset
Bu there's one thing, you bet
This poem is not about me
Or my generation, as you can see
But cricket joins a lot of children
And people of my generation
I think cricket is cool
It's a lot better than pool
It's the game that is the best
Easily better than the rest.

Charlie Tudball (12)
Minehead Middle School, Minehead

My Passion

I love to dance
I spend all my time doing so
I do ballet, tap and street
Soon I wish to do tango

I do my own dance class
They all enjoy a good laugh
We hope to show a dance soon
To all the happy staff

This is why I love to dance.

Jade de Ste Croix (12)
Minehead Middle School, Minehead

Down At The Beach

I lie on the hot sand
It makes you want to sleep
As it burns at your hand
The sea washing over your feet
And your friend comes
That you arranged to meet
You blow up you lilo to go for a dip
As you have a sip of orange
Before you have your dip
That's only a dream
That makes you want to scream
Your baby is crying
Your husband is smiling
The sea is freezing
And you start sneezing
You won't find a beach
Like in my dream.

Leanne White (12)
Minehead Middle School, Minehead

The Barn Owl

As silent as the night,
As swift as the breeze,
As white as the snow
And as smooth as the seas.

His talons as sharp as razors,
His eyes as round as spoons,
His feathers as soft as silk
And his prey stands watching the moon.

Sam Fox (12)
Minehead Middle School, Minehead

Talkin' 'Bout My Generation - West Ham United

Bobby Moore, World Cup winner, sixty-six
James Collins defends the gap between the sticks
Greaves always shot them home

Deano is said to be his clone

It's always been claret and blue
Every three years the shirt is new
About blowing bubbles the fans will sing

My generation hasn't changed a thing

Eggert is the man in charge
Curbishly is quite large
Upton Park is the ground
West Ham the club is quite sound

Named after him
The Bobby Moore stand

West Ham United are the best club in the land!

Luke Cutler (12)
Minehead Middle School, Minehead

Generation

New buildings are built.
Bigger buildings, in and out.

Small children play around.
Teenagers hanging out everywhere.

More babies coming out.
More population, people.

Ignoring world's warning.
Global warming.

Algene Gascon (12)
Minehead Middle School, Minehead

Talkin' 'Bout Me Generation

People always put us down
Talkin' 'bout me generation
Just because we eat badly
Talkin' 'bout me generation
Me mum lives one place, me dad lives another
Talkin' 'bout me generation
Dangerous dog in the street
Talkin' 'bout me generation
Wondering who England can beat
Talkin' 'bout me generation
Council knockin' bike track down
Talkin' 'bout me generation
Ta make place for a borin' shop
Talkin' 'bout me generation
Nothin' for the kids to do
Talkin' 'bout me generation
So street corners will have to do
Talkin' 'bout me generation.

Jacob Jordan (13)
Minehead Middle School, Minehead

Talkin' 'Bout My Generation

Who am I? I don't know
Is my family still alive? I couldn't tell you
What's my name? I try to remember but I can't
Have I got a house, a car or a job? My life is muddled up
Have I got friends or even a girlfriend?
I can't tell you, my past has faded away
Am I in love? I can't seem to find what I had
Who am I? What am I?
I think I'm lost.

Tom Reed (12)
Minehead Middle School, Minehead

Talkin' 'Bout My Generation

My family
Are important to me,
I love all three,
Apart from my aunty.

I don't like her,
Because she likes fur,
She never lets me have chocolate
And she gave me a stupid locket.

My brother is alright,
But he talks all night,
He doesn't bother me,
When he is climbing a tree.

I like my mum,
Even though she stays in the sun,
She is always there,
But sometimes she gives me a scare.

I like my dad,
He isn't bad,
He gives me money,
Even when it's sunny.

Abbie Webber (12)
Minehead Middle School, Minehead

What Am I?

You all made me,
I get hotter,
I cause disaster,
I melt ice caps,
The water around is rising,
Only you can stop me,
I'm just getting worse,
What am I?

Global warming.

Tom Coward (12)
Minehead Middle School, Minehead

Blackpool

Blackpool is very fun,
The theme park has a fun scale of about a ton.
The Ice Blast shoots up and down,
Infusion makes you feel like you found a hundred pound.
The Big One, the biggest in Britain,
So scary, you'd have to strangle your kitten.
Up and down the Eye goes,
Spinning round, you can't see your toes.
The Racing Derby, faster than fast,
You can barely see people walking past.
The ghost train is the scariest that's true,
With werewolves jumping out I go cuckoo.
Blackpool is definitely best by far,
Even if you have to get there by car.

Ciaran Barker (11)
Minehead Middle School, Minehead

In My Life

Me and my family
Have big parties all night long,
Sleeping next day all day long.
Dressing up with fancy clothes,
High heels and long robes.
Going into town,
Buying lots of sweets for the day,
That makes me sick, sometimes.
Surfing at St Ives,
On a sunny day,
The waves are bigger than me,
Going over the waves and under.
Sand all over me!
Going home to have a bath and drink,
Now time for bed!

Gracie Legg (11)
Minehead Middle School, Minehead

Our World

You are what we live on
And what we feed from

You are full of happiness
But become sadness

When the people hurt you
They never know

The next day you could be gone
But they would never see

There's only one
And one only

As in a girl's poem
People might see

We need to take care of you
You might be the last we see

The world is our home
So treat it with respect

I end this poem with a smile
So smile and the world will too

Katie Beauchamp (13)
Minehead Middle School, Minehead

My Brothers

I have two brothers that are in their teens,
I wish they were nicer because they're always mean.
I bet everyone out there with a brother,
Has a brother who is like no other.
They hit and kick,
They're all the same,
I wish I never got the blame.
But you might as well love 'em,
There's no shame.

Jess Lovegrove (12)
Minehead Middle School, Minehead

My Generation

My generation explains 'bout me,
About this world and reality.
All the things I'm going to say
You might see in another way.
I like sport, computers too,
Cars 'n' bikes and lots more woohoo,
I like pasta Bolognese,
There are sometimes good or bad days.
I like playing rugby as a sport,
I hate it when we have to get taught.
Kids can sometimes never think.
Especially when some can stink.
Without friends I could not live,
Apart from some that act like divs.
I like technology when it works,
But sometimes I can go berserk.

Joshua Chilcott (11)
Minehead Middle School, Minehead

My Generation

My stepsister,
She's not good or bad,
Sometimes I wish I could be glad.

She can be kind and funny,
But sometimes she tries to get my money,
We sit at home eating our tea,
Sometimes we even watch TV!

We do lots of things together,
Sometimes it feels like forever,
Me and her are very close,
We sometimes play games, but we love
Listening to music the most.

Lea Blackford (12)
Minehead Middle School, Minehead

Football Days

Some games are easy
And some hard
Sometimes you win
And sometimes you lose
Maybe a penalty
Both ways
You may win by 7 to 0
But then again it could be the other way round
Finally you come on, maybe you score
And maybe you don't
Then the final whistle goes
Maybe you win
Maybe you draw
And maybe you lose.

Kyran Wilkins (12)
Minehead Middle School, Minehead

My Generation

I'm from '07
It's nothing like Heaven

We sit on the sofa
Watching TV

There's nothing going on
Let's go on the PS3

Completed the game
Onto the laptop

Chatting online, bored as can be
Taking to people who are Vietnamese

This is a day from '07
It's certainly *not* like Heaven.

Michael Graddon (12)
Minehead Middle School, Minehead

Penguins And Polar Bears

Polar bears are fluffy
and penguins are fun,
people like to kill them, with a gun,
they do it for their skin, it's just not right,
that's why I'm gonna,
Fight!
Fight!
Fight!

Penguins like to swim and catch fish,
even though they can't eat out of a dish,
their skin is smooth, yeah, they're so cool,
they're funny little creatures, they're so small.

Polar bears are cuddly, they're good to hug,
they dig out nests so they can be snug,
they live in the Arctic, yes they do,
they don't even have one little shoe,
they have fur so they can be warm,
they make their own homes so they can hide from a storm.

So penguins and polar bears are so cool,
Now you know all about them.
They like to play football!

Sam Small (13)
Minehead Middle School, Minehead

The Death Of Conversation

It's mid 1927, conversation's up in Heaven
Reason is the telly's on, no one talks just laughs along.
You offer round the biscuit tin,
There's no response, the air is thin.
I'm moving on ten years or so,
Talk has died
So long ago.

Thomas Strachan (12)
Minehead Middle School, Minehead

The World At Its End

Roses are brown
Violets are down
Everything's dying
So I'm off to town.

Fumes in the air
Now everything's bare
By the roadside
There is a dead hare.

Board games are dead
But electricity has spread
Street lamps are up
And I've got a duck.

I've got and electric sack
And there is war in Iraq
I am pretty bored
So let's praise the Lord.

Scott Gurnett (12)
Minehead Middle School, Minehead

My Generation

This is my family tree
And at the end it is me.
Before comes my mother
And then lots of others.

I have a weird brother,
I think he gets it from my mother.
Maybe somewhere in the tree,
There is someone just like me.

But let's not forget my dad,
Although I think he's pretty mad.
There is also my lovely cat
And I'll never forget that.

Charlotte Williams (12)
Minehead Middle School, Minehead

The World Needs Saving, We Are The Ones To Do It

What have you done to the world?
Litter dropped on grass verges at the sides of the streets.
Sitting on sofas and munching on crisps.
People afraid to go out at night.
What is the world coming to?
It's getting hotter and hotter; the waters are rising, like a monster awaking from a long, deep snooze.
People are getting fatter -
Gnawing on sweets and junk food.
Exercise is becoming unheard of.
What is happening here?
Litter is coating the world, like the wrapping on a present.
We've got to stop this now!
We've got to save the planet for the next generation.
It's down to everyone,
Even you!

Rebecca Willmetts (12)
Minehead Middle School, Minehead

Me And My Generation

TVs blaring out everywhere
Computer screens on
Mobile phones going off
PS2s on the go, PS3s hey ho
Streets are bare, like school upon a weekend
Children spend their hard earned cash
Yeah right, they'd rather fight on the Nintendo Wii
Than spend their weekend with their family.

William Daughtrey (11)
Minehead Middle School, Minehead

My Generation

This is my poem about my generation
I hope this gives a lot of inspiration.
All the things you are about to read,
Are about me, oh yes, indeed!
You will find out about the world
and lots more too
You will find out that cows go moo.
The cool things about life are
technology and sport.
But I don't like it when people start
the next world war.
Life is not always fair,
Like when you run out of underwear.
I think people can be stupid,
Like people that believe in Cupid.
People can be silly, like when they shout,
At you, willy nilly.
I hope you like my poem,
But now I must be goin'.

Thomas Clegg (11)
Minehead Middle School, Minehead

What Is Going On Out There?

Rabbits are hopping
People are snoring
Hear the children sing.

Trees are waving
Conkers are falling
Hear the wind blow.

Fires are burning
Water is spurting
Hear the people scream.

So what is going on out there?

Hamish Cuthbertson (11)
Minehead Middle School, Minehead

My Generation

This is a poem about my generation.
I will tell you about the great sensation.
Well, all these things I'm about to say,
All sorts of people will think of them in a different way.
My life revolves round different things,
Like technology and pigs with wings.
As you can see, kids can think,
But also we can really stink.
Cool things are like bikes and computers,
But old people shout when you ride on your scooters.
I like playing rugby as a sport,
But it does not help when I get caught.
Cricket is cool, I like that the most,
And my favourite foods are pasta and toast.
Chelsea is the best football team,
But when they rarely lose, I jump, shout and sometimes scream.
Well, I'm coming to the end of my poem,
Because I'm a kid and I am growin'.
So to end the poem, I have to say,
I might see you again but in a different way.

Richie Lethaby (11)
Minehead Middle School, Minehead

The Simpsons

These guys are a riot of yellow
Bart Simpson's a bit of a fellow!
He rides a skateboard, showing his bum
And he's always hard work for his dad and his mum.

Here's Homer with three hairs on his head
Marge doesn't want him to be so well fed
She tried to make a difference about his beer
She poured it down the sink
While he was out hunting deer.

Bosko Reynolds (11)
Minehead Middle School, Minehead

My Spring

I think of spring like
A big, fat, juicy pike
I think of the swallows singing to the sea
And a fresh, new pod of peas
The whistling birds on the tops of trees
The buzzing of the newborn bees
The cows ,mooing for the newborn calves
And the fresh bread, cut in halves
The loud noise of a massive splash as we go into the pool
And hammering of all the tools
The cats hissing at the dogs
And the brand new hogs
And the people snoring
And the spring rain pouring
The birds crying for food from their mother
And a kissing pair of lovers
But the best thing
Is the loud din.

Samuel Sparks (11)
Minehead Middle School, Minehead

What If . . . ?

What would happen if the sea was green
And all of the grass was blue?

And if fleas were the size of me and you
And up in the sky the pigs all flew?

Just imagine all the monkeys gibbering and jabbering
The cats all going kaboom!

What if all the dinosaurs came back to us
And wheeled around on roller skates? Zoom!

The world would be mad, crazy, absurd!

I don't think I would live there
But what about you?

Tara Howard (11)
Minehead Middle School, Minehead

Talking About My Generation

The Earth's warming up
But why?
And how?
What's happening to our world?
Oceans warming
Sea levels rising
Ice caps melting
What's happening to our world?
Oil running out
Drought and fires
Floods are common
What can we do?
We need to recycle
We need to use less fuel
Save electricity
What can we do?

*Save the planet
And help our world
To become a better place.*

Abigail Smith (12)
Minehead Middle School, Minehead

People And Things

Trees are falling
People walking
Rabbits hopping
Balls being chucked.

Diggers going
Legs are falling
Taps running
Argh!

The bell has gone
Children walking
On a Friday night.

Charlene Kendall (12)
Minehead Middle School, Minehead

Fifty Pence

When he was a child he lived with his mum
And her boyfriend's gun
One night he went to his uncle's house
His mum and her boyfriend hadn't gone out
They were alone and she got tragically burnt alive
When he came back he saw the house burning with fire
He was angry with everyone
He wished he had a gun
He went out to America, to a ghetto
They treated him like a weirdo
Punched him, hurt him, until the boyfriend came with his gun
And those gangsters lost their fun
He said, 'Why do you have a gun?'
'Just get in the car, Curtis.'
'Not before you tell me, why you have a gun?'
'Just get in the car.'

Luke Senior (11)
Minehead Middle School, Minehead

My Hallowe'en

Zombies, witches, vampires and ghosts
Have some sweets
Who's got the most?

Put all your sweets in a pile
Then dive in
And make it worthwhile

Hallowe'en, Hallowe'en
My best time of year
Eating sweets
Oh, I love it, so dear!

Sarah Clegg (11)
Minehead Middle School, Minehead

Boys

Boys, boys, we're so much better
We're so lazy, we won't read a letter
All of us have a buddy
And together we get very muddy
We won't help in the house
All we do is get rid of a mouse
At school it's the worst
Maths and homework, it's a curse
On Monday it's drama, great!
Then again PE, makes you lose lots of weight
Finally it's Friday, hip hip hooray
We can't wait till the end of the day
On Saturday we've got a match
Quick! Quick! Keeper try and catch
After that it's up the park
And play footie till it's dark
On Sunday it's a bore
I want football, more, more, more
Then again it's back to school
Try and fun is the number one rule!

Billy Stove (11)
Minehead Middle School, Minehead

My Spring Poem

I think of spring as the leaves drop off the trees,
As the newborn of the bees.
I think of spring as the birds find a new home,
I can hear everything except for the gnomes.
I can hear the drips coming off trees,
I can feel nothing except for a breeze.
As you see the squirrels climb through the grass,
You can see the children getting ready for class.

Jessica Griffiths (11)
Minehead Middle School, Minehead

My Generation

The youth.
The youth of today misuse words.
Gay is an insult,
Beast is a compliment,
And women are sometimes called birds.

The nation.
The nation of today is in constant paranoia.
Bird flu,
Smallpox,
Allergies such as soya.

Technology.
Technology today is over used,
In your house,
In your school,
Making adults confused.

Josh Law (13)
Minehead Middle School, Minehead

My Generation

When you are in year 5, 6, 7, or 8
Things will change
You have to relate.

When you go to school
You need to be bold not shy
You will have assembly in the hall
But don't cry.

When you move up to year 9, 10, 11 and 12
It will get a lot harder
Deeper you must delve
To understand?

Bethany Hobbs (11)
Minehead Middle School, Minehead

Sad, Sad Lion

Your mane is short, scruffy and cut,
Unlike when you loved to strut.
Your nose is drying, hour by hour,
In the jungle there was no Big Ben tower.

Drenched in misery, with a broken heart,
But you used to be able to leap and dart.
You used to climb the old trees,
Instead you look at humans' knees.

Two paces wide, your cage is small,
In another cage, there is a lonely call.
People visit, they stop and stare,
Though you get the occasional glare.

The sun is glaring, too hot to bear,
The shade gives loving, loving care.
The roaring of engines, as cars come by,
You still the piercing pain in your thigh.

Your food is prepared, you cannot hunt,
You still think the run was a fantastic stunt.
Stuck in your cage, you wish you could die,
'Cause in the jungle you never did cry.

Jake Thompsett (11)
Minehead Middle School, Minehead

Rugby

Rugby is fun because of the scrum
The lineout is cool because of the ball
I'm covered in muck, stuck in the ruck
My eyes are focussed on the tries
I dreamt the team had Jonny Wilkinson in it
Jonny scored a conversion from the other end
The world's best player broke his leg.

Kieran Williams-Carr (11)
Minehead Middle School, Minehead

It's Great But Annoying

It's fun being a child
Because I have lots of friends,
When I leave school
I still don't want it to end.
When I get home I am all alone
So my friends I phone.
When me and my friends fall out
We shout,
But we soon make friends again.
The SATs are great because it educates you,
But it is annoying.
It's great being a child
But only for a while!

Sophie Morton (11)
Minehead Middle School, Minehead

My Family Tree

Roses are red
Violets are blue
The sun is hot
And so are you.

Roses are red
Violets are blue
My family
Is best in the west.

Toby Kerslake (11)
Minehead Middle School, Minehead

Swim

Gliding through the water,
Swimming like a dolphin,
Up, down, up, down.

Splashing through the water,
Playing like a dolphin,
Up, down, up, down.

Twirling through the water,
Diving like a dolphin,
Up. down. Up, down,
Up, down.

Hannah Norman (11)
Minehead Middle School, Minehead

Grabbist Hill

As I walked upon the hills
I turned around to spectacular views.
My mind kept thinking how wonderful it was,
As in my own world I felt magically lost.
It was so silent and peaceful
As I looked over the hills of the people.
As I strolled along the stony path
I saw in front the shimmering grass.
When I walked along with Mum and my dog
I suddenly realised how clever it was.
To create the beautiful and the soul of the people,
Grabbist Hill.

Danimay Palmer (10)
Minehead Middle School, Minehead

It's Fun But Hard

It's fun being a child
I can run and be wild
I have lots of friends
We play and we don't want it to end
We have lots of fun all day long
And when I go home I listen to my favourite song
It's hard being a child, we do lots of SATs,
It's hard to understand why we have to do that
When I am home
My friends give me a phone
And we go shopping
On our own.

Sophie Coates (11)
Minehead Middle School, Minehead

Me And My Bike

I was on my bike
Riding through the pine trees
With mud puddles everywhere.

I was on my bike
Riding up a hill
I felt so tired and had to chill.

I was on my bike
Riding through the streets
Going to the BMX track
To meet my peeps.

Brandon Scarlett (11)
Minehead Middle School, Minehead

Friends

F riends are nice to you when you're down
R eckon they're the best out of the gang in town
I n school they help you do your work
E nding a friendship is so hard, so don't break up
N ever forget your old friends
D on't forget their number.

Reem Nicholls (11)
Minehead Middle School, Minehead

My Gran

Talkin' 'bout my generation
My generation
I could talk about a skating gran
But I'm not going to
Instead I'm going to talk about a horse riding gran
She taught me how to ride
My horse riding gran is amazing
It's really funny when she canters
My gran is the best gran

Ellie-May Murphy (11)
Minehead Middle School, Minehead

Prime Ministers

Prime ministers suck, so do politicians,
I think they have special conditions.
Gordon took over from Tony Blair,
Only because he was losing his hair.
To the country I thought he was unfair,
So I'm glad that Brown took over from Blair.

Jack Thake (13)
Minehead Middle School, Minehead

Teenage Years

Teenage years are stressful and sad,
Boyfriends and girlfriends make you mad.
Fashions and hairstyles, plus lots and lots,
Of great, fat, ugly spots.

Teenage years are long and scary,
Armpits get sweaty, legs get hairy,
Exams come round and stress you out,
Loads of teachers moan and shout.

Teenage years are full of glee and pleasure,
You're out the house at your own leisure!
Counted as an adult but also a child,
At your friend's party you can all go wild!

In teenage years there's always something great,
They may seem bad, but just you wait -
Once you get through all the annoying friends,
Got rid of the blues and conquered the trends,
You'll have learnt from the bad times that made you feel low,
You'll be experienced, ready and raring to go!

Frances Hamblin (12)
St John's School & Community College, Marlborough

What Do They Know?

'Get out of bed!'
they call.
'It's time for school!'
they bellow.
They think we're all lazy and whiny,
All we do is eat and sleep.
But it's not true,
We worry, we care.
Are we going to pass our maths test?
What homework do we have to do?

'Be quiet, sit down!'
they bark.
'You are in science, not the circus!'
they shout.
When they think you're chatting,
But actually, you're discussing the lesson.
They accuse us of wearing make-up,
But you really aren't.
We're accused and accused,
They just don't believe us.
We're not in bed because we're hiding,
We're just tired.
We aren't daydreaming,
We're thinking deeply.
But what do they know?
They're not us . . .

Ruby Tucker (12)
St John's School & Community College, Marlborough

Life

Life is a funny thing you see,
Has lots of choices,
Hmmm, coffee or tea?
Is it set out in certain paths?
Choosing certain ones
Can mean arguments or laughs.
Is it a big long road
With problems that arise?
You can be famous or quiet
And maybe just hide.
Does it depend on your family or what you buy?
Or is it really how hard you try?
What happens when you die?
Do you come back as something else?
You could come back as a tree
And be carved into a shelf.
Does time tick away,
Or is each day the same?
Should you make the most of them,
Or play them like a game?
No one knows
Really what and where we are.
So in the end,
Life's a bag of sweets.
Pick out and choose,
What life you may lead.

Hannah Beard (13)
St Katherine's School, Bristol

Fear - All Our Lives

The long, straight way home,
The finish to a bad time,
The road full of fear,
Nowhere to go but the slow lane.

Others speed along and overtake,
Whilst I try to stay away,
From the end of the road,
Where I am scared to be.

I make it very close,
Merely 100 yards away,
I cross the end of the line,
And then need to start again.

Ben Harris (14)
The Crypt School, Gloucester

Mash Potatoes

Happiness is like a big bowl of mashed potatoes,
All soft and loveable,
It leaves a lovely feeling in your stomach,
But have too much, it can leave you sick.

It begins hard,
But with good work and love it turns out delicious,
But watch out, it can be vicious,
It sometimes has problems and lumps its suspicious.

Happiness is like a big bowl of mashed potatoes,
All soft and loveable.

James Weaver (14)
The Crypt School, Gloucester

The Killer Mole

You dig deep into my being,
You crawl under my skin,
I feel like I'll never win,
What have I done to sin?

The pain I feel is not of my own,
It feels like my head is exploding,
As you burrow deeper and deeper,
The pain grows more and more.

Holes in my being have been left by you,
I feel empty like a hole,
It feels like I have no soul,
All this pain has taken its toll,
You are a killer mole.

Ryan Dunne (14)
The Crypt School, Gloucester

Boredom

You are plainer than paper,
Duller than Death's funeral,
It creeps up everywhere,
You can't miss it.

It is darkness,
It is a blank wall,
Seep away the colours,
From pictures of the past.

What is life without it?
It makes you do things new,
No colour,
Nothing interesting.

Bradley Pring (14)
The Crypt School, Gloucester

Rock

A rock is a rock,
As strong as an ox,
But what does it do?

Well nothing at all,
That's what,
A rock is a rock.

It can't express its feelings,
Or make love either,
It's just a potato,
But harder that's all.

A rock is a rock,
That's all, nothing more,
Can't do anything.

What fun!
Not.

Ben Dowd (14)
The Crypt School, Gloucester

Fury

Like the heat of a chilli,
Fury starts small,
Growing to an enormous size,
And releasing with energy.

Your face turns red and
Your eyes fill with water,
Even a tiny bit hurts,
Like the heat of a chilli.

Chris Silk (14)
The Crypt School, Gloucester

Me . . .

In 1995, I became alive,
On a warm spring day in March,
As I began to grow, my life started to flow,
I had begun life's arch.

At the age of 4, I discovered school,
In September was my first day,
When I reached Year 7, I was only 11,
To Crypt I was on my way.

My first week I was rather scared,
Making new friends was quite hard,
As time went past, my friends started to last,
Although some friendships got scarred.

Here I am now,
Writing this poem,
Thinking what to say about what happened today,
As my childhood is going.

Ben Simmonds (12)
The Crypt School, Gloucester

Pain

Pain, it spreads like fire,
It's feared like fire,
It's red like fire,
It hurts like fire,
It is fire,
The bringer of pain,
The blistering heat,
The scolding touch,
Fire.

Josh Myrans (14)
The Crypt School, Gloucester

It's Try Time

The ball is the shape of an egg,
You tackle them around the leg,
Flankers or number eights,
Your team are your mates.

Props and hookers are beasts,
Their pre-match meals are feasts,
Second rows are over 6 feet,
They are a giant piece of meat.

The halfbacks are the wizards,
Their up and unders fly with the birds,
A penalty in front of the posts,
A 50 yarder he will boast.

The centres work hard,
They try and make the other team look like a retard,
The big tackles or the quick break,
Weave through the defence like a grass snake.

The wingers and full back are very quick,
They pierce the defence like a balloon and a prick,
Clip through the tackles like slime,
They put the ball down and it's try time.

Liam Ward (14)
The Crypt School, Gloucester

Emotion Poem - Relief

Relief is a cool blue sky after a fire,
It is like water after walking through the desert,
It is like a smooth, smooth dolphin when you are lost at sea,
It is like a jeep when you are lost in the jungle,
Or a comfy chair when you have just got home in your jeep,
From being lost in the jungle.

Christian Lange (14)
The Crypt School, Gloucester

Suicide

Hell hath no fury,
For those who step willingly,
Into the abyss,
The dark beyond,
An unknown void,
Endless and all knowing,
The dark beyond,
Holds no surprises,
For those who step willingly,
Into the abyss.

Phil Morgan (15)
The Crypt School, Gloucester

Jealousy

Jealousy is scalding and bright orange,
Boiling up inside,
Burnt by hot tea,
Jealousy is an eagle targeting its prey,
Nooding it more and more,
Laid down on a rusty sofa.

Luke Wildman (11)
The Crypt School, Gloucester

Anger

Anger is acid red,
Burning me alive at 1,920°c,
It is like a sour lemon in my mouth,
It's like Dettol bleach torturing germs,
It is an ever-stinging hornet buzzing around my head,
Burning acid tearing a hole in me,
A raging Lamborghini Murcielago roaring down the road,
It's like a brown sofa left out on the road.

Jack Ashton (11)
The Crypt School, Gloucester

My Generation

Today in this generation,
We are so advanced,
We have super computers,
And iPod Nanos.

All we have to do is press a small button,
And down comes a plasma flatscreen TV,
With surround sound and DVD player,
48 inches.

Now we have PS3s,
That makes it look like you're actually there,
And games that make the people look nearly like us,
And it feels like you're really the character.

Now there are tiny things that can hold over 200 songs,
While back then, they were huge boxes and only held 20,
And although we've got all this good stuff, people keep upgrading,
Why bother it's fine as it is.

Mike Smith (12)
The Crypt School, Gloucester

Fear!

You strike the hearts of everyone,
Pierce the body,
Pierce the heart,
Pierce the soul,
Until you leave the empty shell,
Leave the empty body.
People avoid you,
People resist you,
But you take them by surprise,
You're too fast,
You're too strong,
You invade their body,
And change them forever.

Dan Bannister (14)
The Crypt School, Gloucester

Anger Is . . .

Anger is a rhino,
Calm sometimes and destructive others,
It batters people,
Leaves them hurt.

Anger is a bull,
Leaving a path of devastation,
Like a speeding car in
A big, city - noisy.

Anger is a crocodile,
Snappy and fast,
Completely destroying everything,
You have built.

Dane Nash (11)
The Crypt School, Gloucester

Depression

Depression is a black cloud,
Hanging overhead,
With a sickly scent,
Depression is a staircase,
Climbing up,
Then falling down,
Depression is a pumpkin,
Sold,
Cut,
Lit,
Then put out,
Depression is cold and lonely.

Charlie Williams (11)
The Crypt School, Gloucester

Boredom

Boredom is a grey dull colour boring my brain to death,
Boredom is a 'Health and Safety' talk just when you
Need to get on with something,
Boredom is a council meeting about global warming,
And slower speed limits,
Boredom is a watery taste with the tiniest bit of orange squash,
Boredom is 'Top Gear' without Jeremy Clarkson,
Boredom is a smooth wooden texture,
Boredom is the smell of a just cleaned toilet,
Boredom is a blue Ford Focus,
How boring!

Daniel Charlton (11)
The Crypt School, Gloucester

Stop And Think

They always pick on us, it's unfair,
Just because we do well and care,
The things they are always physical,
I hope they don't see me feeling miserable.

Why, why, why, why, do they do it?
Why can't they stop and think through it?

Why don't you leave us alone?
Please don't take my mobile phone,
You know what I, I just said,
Please don't kick me in the head.

Why, why, why, why do they do it?
Why can't they stop and think through it?

Adam Crabbe (12)
The Crypt School, Gloucester

Sadness

Sadness is a slow turtle,
Never reaching its destination,
It is a cold rusty car,
That is never used,
Sadness is a cold, unforgettable smell,
That looms over you forever,
It is black, bitter lemons,
Full of sour depression.

Adam Allen (11)
The Crypt School, Gloucester

Confusion

Confusion is like yellow stars going round my head,
It's cold enough to make your brain freeze and stop working,
It's like a pear, is it a squashed apple or a pear?
It's like milk and orange mixed,
A funny smell tickling my nose,
Goes liquid to solid like jelly,
It is like a chameleon changing your colour inflicting your mind,
It's like a car spinning out of control.

Max Williams (11)
The Crypt School, Gloucester

Boredom

Boredom is white, room temperature,
An old nut,
It is like warm squash,
A stale smell,
It's completely smooth,
It's like an old sloth,
It's a red old Hyundai,
It's a plain wooden chair.

Jordan Hopwood (11)
The Crypt School, Gloucester

My Generation

There's always someone on my generation's back,
They need to get off or nothing will be done,
With tight deadlines there's no slack,
Leave me alone and get off my back!

We are the generation of the Internet,
People say we are slobs and lazy,
I learn about people from their blogs,
Older people's opinions are sometimes crazy.

Mums and dads think they know what's best,
Always on my back and poking on my chest,
I do my best to please everybody,
But need my time and space for me.

We like to laugh and talk on MSN,
Swap ideas through wires and lines,
Laugh at videos on YouTube,
It's great, everybody else should.

Our life is ours, stop interfering,
Let me get on with it and be myself,
Put your old opinions back on the shelf,
This generation belongs to us!

Matthew Hunter (12)
The Crypt School, Gloucester

Anger

Anger is hot and red, burning my skin,
Scalding in bubbling lava,
While toasting a marshmallow,
Like your life turning back,
I feel down as my blood drips down my face,
Into my mouth, I swallow it down my throat,
The ants just won't stop crawling around,
On my body the pain sends millions of shivers
Down my spine . . .

Edward Plant (11)
The Crypt School, Gloucester

Excitement

Excitement is bright and bold like fire,
It's moderate until it suddenly flares up,
It's tropical and sweet,
Petrol flaring up when fire touches it,
The spicy smell of curry,
It's never flat but always bumpy,
A tiger ready to pounce,
An Aston Martin roaring down the road,
A swivel chair always moving.

Harry McDowell (12)
The Crypt School, Gloucester

Aggressive

The colour of aggressive, a red and hint of black,
Is a coloured lion ready to jump out,
The temperature at boiling,
Is at the mark to take it out on anything.

The texture of cracked lines,
Is fierce like on the tiger for killing,
The drink of Red Bull,
Is fuming up for hatred.

Matthew Wilkinson (11)
The Crypt School, Gloucester

Love

Love is a pink swan,
It is a warm hot tub that bubbles like champagne,
It is a warm smooth chocolate that you eat in a fast convertible,
It's the smell of perfume running up your nose,
Love is together, forever.

Tom Beckett (11)
The Crypt School, Gloucester

Roundabout Youth

On the island sat two rabbits
Basking in the sun,
The first turned to the other one
And asked from whence they'd come.

Quite bemused lay rabbit two,
Wiggling his pink nose:
Around him his own questions drove
Of which his squeaks gave pose.

'Should I expand my burrow,
With a mortgage loan?
Do I have enough carrots,
For them to financially condone?'

With raised ears, ruffled fur,
Agitation grew,
Until, at last, across the road,
Came God missing half a shoe.

On her lap she gathered them up,
Fell asleep smiling at the sky,
Never to tyres will the rabbits lose,
Though the rabbits try.

James Robertson (17)
The Crypt School, Gloucester

Anger

Anger is boiling hot,
Its red hot lava erupting from a volcano brings
The horrible smell of smoke to your nose,
It's spikier than a pineapple piercing your skin,
It's more painful than running your hand across
Barnacles at a beach,
It's the deafening sound of a lion roaring close up,
It's thicker than metal on a garbage truck,
It's constant annoyance of sitting on a hard wooden stool for hours.

Theo Tibbs (11)
The Crypt School, Gloucester

Talkin' 'Bout My Generation

Since I was small, a lot has changed,
We all have mobile phones,
Games consoles and Internet,
Yet everyone still moans!

My generation understands,
What WAP and Bluetooth mean,
How to play game consoles,
And view computer screens.

We all must try to recycle,
As much stuff as we can,
Old refrigerators, ovens, bags,
But most importantly Coke cans.

Global warming is a risk,
Too many different things,
Polar bears, seals, Arctic foxes,
And of course, penguins.

The population is rising!
Especially in China,
The skies are filled with jumbo jets,
The seas awash with liners.

Josh Downham (11)
The Crypt School, Gloucester

Anger

Anger is a submarine,
It travels down deep to your heart,
Cold and hard,
It escalates higher.

It needs more than one to work,
Things you never knew can be found,
The pressure rises the further you go,
Until many things begin to break and slow.

Marty Fisk (11)
The Crypt School, Gloucester

My Generation

We like to throw parties, all to have fun,
They say we're not allowed acting like our God,
They say instead it's better to learn,
We think it's all unfair they get to do what they want.

We like peace and quiet and have some wine,
But they yell, they scream saying they're having fun,
They think it's unfair not to be able to stay up late,
But we think it's better if they stayed in at night.

Outside there are guns and crimes,
And if they go out there, they'll probably have a fright,
The local gangs threaten them but they don't want to share,
We think this is all wrong and that the police should help.

The gangs on the streets, they scare us,
Asking us to join them and to rob a house,
They like to start a fight, they make themselves feel supreme,
And they only do this to get back at their parents.

This is our generation,
Lots of wars and crime, we can't really stop it,
But with your help we might.

Ben Gribble (13)
The Crypt School, Gloucester

Talkin' 'Bout My Generation

I hate it when my grandparents talk about their day,
They're talking about their farm and all the hay,
I wish that when I go round their house,
They could just give me a drink,
But instead they just go and clean the old sink,
They sit there and talk about the war,
I sit there and think what a bore,
When I get older, I hope I'm not the same,
Otherwise I'll drive you all insane.

Liam Walsh (12)
The Crypt School, Gloucester

Talkin' About My Generation

People say we watch too much television,
When we could be learning multiplication and division.

Now there is too much war,
With blood and gore,
Kids on violent games,
Then setting cars to flames,
People driving way too fast,
Like this they will not last,
It's all bad on the news,
About people on drugs and booze,
People don't speak right,
And hang around at night,
They are always on the phone,
And if you talk to them, they will just groan,
The generations are getting worse and worse,
You better keep your hand on your purse.

People say we watch too much television,
When we could be learning multiplication and division.

Leigh Smith (12)
The Crypt School, Gloucester

Anger

Anger is black,
Anger is hot, boiling hot,
It smells like methane and tastes like acid,
It is rough, like slipping on rocks,
It buzzes around like a bluebottle,
It's worse than driving an old Ford Anglia whilst
                            you've got constipation.

Anger,
It is like an olive,
Black and bitter.

Josh Williams (12)
The Crypt School, Gloucester

Bully

Bully, no single person is worth these tears
That flow and tear me apart,
No single person is worth these tears
That flow when you start,
Bully, the flame that glows will not go out,
You are here,
The flame that glows will not go out,
You are fear,
No single person is worth these tears,
That flow and that flame that glows to break my heart!

Katie Wedgbury (16)
The Crypt School, Gloucester

Jealousy

Jealousy is cold, green and uncaring,
The cause of breaking relationships,
Unwanted but still, it advances,
It lives in everyone, hidden but living,
Ready to rise at any time.

People try to stamp it out,
But it keeps coming,
Growing and gaining strength,
Until it overwhelms you,
And you cannot resist it any longer.

James Clifford (15)
The Crypt School, Gloucester

Talkin' 'Bout My Generation

The kids these days are useless,
They just want to have fun,
If you give them a strawberry bun,
They will shoot you with a gun.

But we are not all like that,
Most people think we are,
When some try to nick a Mars Bar,
They're driven off in a car.

Bradley Meredith (12)
The Crypt School, Gloucester

My Generation

Football in the morning,
TV at night,
Watching horror movies just for a fright,
Adults are really bossy, telling you what to do,
It's really annoying when they think they are just like you,
Going to school,
It's so boring,
Sitting through a lecture,
Falling asleep and snoring.

Mike Payne (12)
The Crypt School, Gloucester

Talking 'Bout My Generation

People try to make us frown,
People try to take us down,
People hate us having fun,
People think we are really dumb,
They ruin a generation!

Elders hate us every day,
They just want us to die away,
Sometimes people are scared of us,
They wish we were a speck of dust,
They ruin a generation!

Most people's generation is ruined,
But people's generation are just stewing,
God protects us every day,
All they think they are doing is child's play,
They ruin a generation!

We all pull through even if we are hurt,
Or even with a scratch on the shirt,
We all hate people who sit and stare,
And all they say is 'Don't you dare!'
They ruin a generation.

Now all done is done,
All we want to do is have some fun!

Aaron Smith (12)
The Crypt School, Gloucester

My Generation

My generation is an amazing thing,
Like PlayStation, Xbox, a lot of bling,
Massive TVs and laptops are cool,
With colour screens and watching the football,
Having iPods and MP3s to keep us musically entertained,
Wanting the newest stuff, we can't be blamed,
Having mobile phones are the latest trend,
Phones with a cord would drive me round the bend.

My generation is really cool,
All this technology would make you drool.

Elderly people complain and curse,
'All these rebels are getting worse',
Not understanding that most of us aren't bad,
It's because their minds are failing, it's quite sad,
Having simple stuff is hard for us,
If we don't get the latest stuff, then we make a fuss,
They give us tea and biscuits and I'm grateful,
But what we need is high-energy drinks and sweets by the plateful.

My generation is really cool,
If you don't like sweets, then you're considered a fool,
My generation . . .

James Stevens (12)
The Crypt School, Gloucester

Unspoken Words

A baby sits and stares,
Yearning for its poison,
A ghost reliving its death,
Waiting for the light.

Plastic chains constrict it,
Rubber tubing silences it,
Its dreams, its hopes, its aspirations,
The trampled teddy in the grit.

Its cries never cease,
They echo the pain of hell,
It would consume a mortal man,
Leaving but a hollow shell.

Its owners stand remorseless,
Impervious to its suffering,
Their icy glares boring in,
Branding its soft, tender skin.

As thought evolves a light flicks on,
Brighter by the second,
A bundle of life and joy,
Begins to unfold.

Gradually it rises,
Beyond the soulless dungeons,
To the surface of the world,
Beneath the glowing sun.

Ben Rhodes (14)
The Crypt School, Gloucester

Talkin' 'Bout My Generation

Young and old,
Long and bold.

Apartments and homes,
Brushes and combs.

TV and radio,
Guitar and piano.

Shower and bath,
Volunteer and maths.

Bowls and football,
Short and tall.

Tim Smith (12)
The Crypt School, Gloucester

What I Used To Do

I used to wear a nappy,
And I used to crawl around,
I was sick upon my mummy,
And I would sit there on the ground.

I used to need a highchair,
I once played with Barbie dolls,
I used to make mud pies,
And my clothes were full of holes!

I once had scruffy handwriting,
And I wanted to know how,
The cogs in the clock worked,
Well, I know the answer now.

But now I'm in Year 7,
I'm eleven and I'm proud,
Reading back upon my poem,
Makes me laugh out loud!

Adele Franghiadi (11)
The High School for Girls, Gloucester

Never Forget The Memories

All the memories we had were shared together,
Because we were best friends forever,
Then the time we had to move on,
It all felt so weird and so wrong.

You've been my best friend since I can remember,
Our own little club and I was a member,
Now we are always apart,
But you'll always be my best friend in my heart.

I remember when we started school,
You were crying and I acted cool,
You've been like my big sister,
Always with me, my silent listener.

Why do things have to change?
Why can't things stay the same?
I can see you at any time,
But not seeing you every day feels like a crime.

I can remember our toddler photos,
You used to cry and I always posed,
When we got older, I would cry,
You'd say - 'It's OK' - that was a lie.

We knew what the other was thinking,
We knew when one's heart was sinking,
A simple smile would cheer one up,
Like twins, peas in a pod, that's us.

One thing we must do,
If you assure me, I assure you!
I will never forget the memories!

Renee James-Bryan (12)
The High School for Girls, Gloucester

My Family

You would expect families to be small, wouldn't you,
But my family is anything but that.

It consists of people of all ages,
From one to one hundred and one!

Some are Christians, some are Jews.

People in my family come from all sorts of
Different backgrounds, some are Italian,
Whilst some are Arabic.

My family speaks lots of different languages,
Some of us speak Japanese, some of us German.

We all have different opinions,
Sometimes we fight for what we think is right,
Resolving in people getting hurt and sometimes even dying.

But there is one thing that makes us all the same,
We're all one big family.

If you can't guess who my family is yet,
I had better just go ahead and tell you . . .
My family is everyone in the world!

Freya Hansen (11)
The High School for Girls, Gloucester

The Vampire

Her hair whipped her face like a tattered kite,

Pale as the moon, dark as night,
Her eyes red as blood,
Black wings ready to open like a flower bud.

She sat back and waited in the moonlight,

Warriors come, warriors go,
Even with the moon so low,
Come to me, my warrior foes,

And I shall show you something that
Makes even the most mighty warriors turn white . . .

Samantha Collins (11)
The High School for Girls, Gloucester

Talkin' 'Bout My Generation

Everything is changing for the best!
I'm making lots of fantastic friends,
And we have long happy half-term holidays,
As my confidence grows, I have more fun,
I join in more, I take part,
But looking the part is important too,
For looking cool is great!

Harry Rogers (13)
West Somerset Community College, Minehead

Talkin' 'Bout My Generation

I was trapped,
In a world of shadows,
I was trapped,
In a world of suspicion.

I was trapped,
In a world of doubt,
I was trapped,
In a world of awareness.

I was trapped,
In a world of hate,
I was trapped,
In a world of paranoia.

A girl howled me out,
And told me to do what I loved,
Which was to smile,
So I did.

The bleak walls fell down,
The light in my eyes,
But I smiled and smiled,
And felt alive.

She laughs in my ear,
She brightens my day,
So I keep my smile,
And now I'm free.

Dawn-Marie Williams (13)
West Somerset Community College, Minehead

Talkin' 'Bout My Generation

People think it's easy,
But,
People don't know,
It's hard,
Tough,
You have to
Study,
Know what's the latest,
Manage your love life,
And,
If you say or do one little thing wrong,
That's it,
It's over,
You're gone.

Alice O'Shea (13)
West Somerset Community College, Minehead

Talkin' 'Bout My Generation

M any people wonder what it's like to be a teen,
Y et every day's the same . . . in school.

G eneration is a time and nothing else,
E veryone nowadays is exactly the same,
N ever changing but time's always moving forward,
E ven now new technology is being invented,
R adiation is so strong, my phone turns off with pressure,
A ll the girls always fall out,
T omorrow half term starts and I can't wait,
I 'll be with my mates for the whole week,
O n days at home, I'm actually out,
N ever am I alone.

Charley Chandler
West Somerset Community College, Minehead

Talkin' 'Bout My Generation

Well this is me,
Emilie,
And that's all I can be,
No more,
No less,
No second guess,
I laugh,
I love,
I live,
I cry,
And some days I wish I would just die,
Sometimes I'm funny,
Others I'm not,
Sometimes in overdrive,
And I just can't stop,
You may not like me,
But that's OK,
This is me,
And this is how I will stay!

Emilie Smith (14)
West Somerset Community College, Minehead

Talking About My Generation

Always bored,
Never adored,
Arguments shake the wall,
That is really uncool,
Cycling fast,
Music on with a blast,
Always hungry, eating stuff,
Never seem to have enough,
In college, homework abounds,
Is even worse than doing paper rounds,
At least I'm earning ten pounds,
How long can I bear it?

Oliver Bartle (13)
West Somerset Community College, Minehead

What About The Title?

Keep running,
From who you are,
Keep running,
From what you've done,
You're playing the game,
You're cheating with dust,
Who are you?
Where are you?
No one to catch you,
No system to dodge,
Nothing special,
Just snow surrounding,
Alone, algid,
Anxious, addicted,
Come back to reality,
Now I know the truth,
It's too far to go back.

Eleanor Stone (15)
West Somerset Community College, Minehead

Talkin' 'Bout My Generation

Being a teenager is kinda cool,
Some of the clowns are fools and school,
Lots of people are dying from disease and war,
Lots of people are really poor,
Lots of people are into trends,
It really drives me round the bend,
A lot of things make me really mad,
Like people consumed by the latest fad,
I hate just sitting at home alone,
I like being out but not on my own,
I have a really good mate,
We think that we met by fate,
All in all, I think it's cool,
All except those fools and school.

Davey Owen
West Somerset Community College, Minehead

Rules And Rights

You should get a job,
You don't get money for doing nothing,
Unless you're the Queen!

Everyone has the right to voice their own opinion,
But only if you're in a position of power.

You should follow what you believe is right,
No one can try and convert you,
Unless that no one's from the BNP.

Everyone has the right to food and water,
With the exception of millions who can't afford it,
Weapons come first.

You should be an individual and not be stereotyped,
Being yourself is a good thing,
Until they start to notice.

Everyone has the right not to be killed,
Killing is a crime,
Unless it is done by a soldier.

Remi Toth (14)
West Somerset Community College, Minehead

Talkin' 'Bout My Generation

All these kids trying to be cool,
But seriously they are such a drawl,
The weed, the booze, the Coke and the fags,
All of them attract the lads,
The girls always get what they need,
But most of it is just weed,
The exams and the stress,
But at least it leads to the prom dress,
Emos are overtaking,
Because of that I start baking.

Grace Wilson (13)
West Somerset Community College, Minehead

Detention

As your mates go out to play,
Stuck inside, you have no say,
A quiet mouth, an untouched pen,
You hope you don't fail here again.

Give evil eyes out to your teacher,
It's all her fault, don't dare preach her,
Another ten minutes, in this confined Hell,
All because you could not spell.

The laughter and gossip goes astray,
Anger builds up cos you don't get your way,
The waiting, the dating,
The friends and the hating.

A place,
Not for the human race,
To your mother not to mention,
But I'll be there, see you in detention.

Francesca Walker (14)
West Somerset Community College, Minehead

Teenagers Today

Dark rainy boring nights,
Sitting round with friends,
Nothing to do,
Too dark to play football,
So we hang around near the shops,
Messing around,
People warily scurry past clutching their bags,
We're not all bad you know,
People are too quick to judge,
We just want some fun and
To be with our friends.

Kieran Parsons (14)
West Somerset Community College, Minehead

Talking About My Generation

Kids of the 90s,
Youth of today,
Brought up on Pingu,
And Barbie as well,
Kids of the 90s,
Youth of today,
Dungarees and doodles,
Jellyshoes and jeans,
Kids of the 90s,
Youth of today,
Tamagotchis and Game Boys,
Our obsession began,
Kids of the 90s,
The youth of today,
Computers and Wiis,
iPods and DVDs,
The square-eyed generation,
The youth of today.

Rebecca Salter (14)
West Somerset Community College, Minehead

Teenage Life

Teenage life with all my friends,
All the trouble never ends,
Homework, essays, never stop,
Teachers shouting chop, chop, chop,
Chilling, playing, listening to tunes,
Going to the park and down the flumes,
Daytime school and extra jobs,
New technology and changing mobs,
Swimming, scrapping, eating food,
The cats just died and Mum's in a mood,
All these cards, grades and marks,
My brother's a weirdo, he just barks.

Nancy McGowan (13)
West Somerset Community College, Minehead

Talking About My Generation

Teenagers,
We all have minds of our own,
We're our own generation,
We're in groups,
But we're all different people.

Teenagers,
Made to go to school,
By the government controlling everybody,
It's such a bore,
But we can't do anything about it.

Teenagers,
We're around every corner,
You can't escape us,
Don't be scared,
We don't bite,
We're just normal people,
Our own generation.

Abbie Davies (14)
West Somerset Community College, Minehead

Untitled

A stage in life where I overtake,
I can learn from my own mistakes,
Overpowering emotion,
Love, hate, complete devotion,
Odd blocks of sadness in my way,
I feel bad and others pay,
A teenager is what I have become,
Often lost and worried, but trying to make survival fun,
A stage in life where I overtake,
With choices to change my life,
That I alone will have to make.

Steff Hartgen (14)
West Somerset Community College, Minehead

Teenagers

Teenagers listen to music,
They fall in love,
They're like doves,
They like their own freedom,
So you should leave them,
They are as fierce as a lion,
The boys might be Dion,
They like to mess about,
And they might be out and about,
They like to have fun,
They don't want to see the sun,
They will be silly
And they act nilly,
The teenagers joke,
And they poke,
If they are not at home,
They are out and hanging around,
They sometimes get depressed,
And they like to moan,
And they don't pay a loan.

Amie Hutchings (13)
West Somerset Community College, Minehead

Gone Forever

They have gone, the only kid in the house,
I feel so lonely, no one else to talk to, bored,
No more play fights,
It feels strange in the way that both my
Brothers have moved and out moved on with their lives,
In the 13 years I have had the smallest room in the house
And now the biggest with a double bed to spread out,
But it feels strange, in the way that I have their old room.

Jack Sully
West Somerset Community College, Minehead

Teenagers

Boys and girls have different problems,
Seeing things in different ways,
Nothing to be ashamed of - it is life,

I have to do the same thing every morning,
Getting up,
Getting dressed,
Having breakfast,
Brushing my teeth,
And chasing the bus,
Going to school, having my lessons,
Going home and doing the same thing
As this morning.

I have my friends, they are fun,
They are there when I want them,
They stick up for me and have a laugh
But most of all, they are my friends.

People can get you into things like
Drugs,
Sex,
Alcohol,
Smoking,
They are only there if you want them,
Don't let people get you into them.

There are different teenagers like
Grebos, emos, chavs and wannabes
People might hate you but
You choose what you want to be.

In the future you decide what you want to be,
Don't let everyone else tell you what to do.

Finlay Bastable
West Somerset Community College, Minehead

Teenagers

Teenagers shout, teenagers swear,
When they get angry, they don't give a care.

Teenagers smoke, teenagers drink,
If they drink too much,
It will be back up in the sink.

Teenagers love music,
It's one of their things,
They drink Red Bull because it gives them wings.

Teenagers are brave, teenagers are strong,
They love a sexy lady wearing a thong.

Teenagers think they're smart,
Think they look cool,
They know it already, who needs school?

Stephen Yard (13)
West Somerset Community College, Minehead

Kayleigh Kendall

K ittens playing in the snow,
A pples falling from the tree,
Y ellow sunshine,
L ittle children playing games,
E ating a picnic by the river,
I cicles falling from the sky,
G reen grass growing,
H orses galloping by.

K ittens playing with wool,
E ggs all runny and yolky,
N ice day for a holiday,
D ads whistling to the music,
A utumn's coming,
L eaves falling from the trees,
L ittle kittens sleeping.

Kayleigh Kendall (13)
West Somerset Community College, Minehead

Teenage Years

Hit thirteen and your life will change,
Mind in a mess, your head in the clouds,
But amongst all insanity,
True meaning is found,
You begin to gain control,
Feet firmly on the ground,
These are the years you learn who you are,
Thus setting the path for your adult days,
Meeting new challenges,
And school becomes tough,
Old friends start to judge you,
And you'll start to feel rough,
But with music I've found,
I can get through it all,
It brings me to new people,
Again I stand tall,
Teenage years, yeah, they can be hard,
But savour the good times,
Best years of your life!

Joe Stileman (14)
West Somerset Community College, Minehead

Teenage Life

Teenage life is pretty cool,
We get treated as grown-ups at school.

I am allowed to wear make-up now,
Without me and my mum getting into a row.

I like riding my pony Brian,
He's all fluffy in the winter like a lion.

Mobile phones are the thing,
Because people decorate them with bling.

Life is OK as a teenager.

Clare Davey (13)
West Somerset Community College, Minehead

Being A Teenager In 2007

T anks begin war,
E ven the small ones,
E veryone is against you,
N othing is fair,
A ngst and sadness,
G etting on your nerves,
E nvironment changing,

Y our fault,
E ver complaining,
A lways,
R ight,
S hut up, you stupid little brat.

Alternative to the above

T anks,
E nemies,
E nvironment,
N ormality,
A nnoyance,
G uilt,
E motions,

Y oung,
E nvious,
A ngst,
R age,
S tupidity.

Jake Dorrill (14)
West Somerset Community College, Minehead

Teenagers Rule

T eens hanging around the streets,
E xtra ordinary lights popping up,
E veryone around scared and cowering in their houses,
N o one will come out with them on the streets,
A ge old men and women *never* leave their houses,
G enes might have passed onto these terrible teens,
E ggs and flour are thrown at Hallowe'en because they
                                                don't get a treat,
R overs pushing through with armed forces inside . . .
S ome of the good teenagers are mistaken for bad.

R ebellions of them around the country,
U nder bridges, over roads,
L eading gangs with knives and guns,
E very teen will soon know.

T hat once one life is shattered, others will as well,
H eroes are needed in this world, not villains,
E ventually the teens will go home and listen to this:

W hy don't they just go home and spend lost time with family,
O rder something, sit down,
R elax
L isten to music,
D ance like no one is watching and . . .
   Never give in.

Briony Flello
West Somerset Community College, Minehead

Untitled

Teenage life in Britain,
Is not well suited to writing poetry,
There are no poetic scenes,
No twinkling of the night sky,
There's rubbish,
And cigarette ends,
iPods,
XBox,
No well-spoken prose to one another,
Notes on the fridge door,
And instant messaging,
Miniature wars between different cultures,
Major and minor,
Black and white,
Teenage life in Britain,
Is not well suited to writing poetry.

Abi Owen (14)
West Somerset Community College, Minehead

Inferior

Look at me when I'm preaching to you
oh, but
all that was needed
from an unconditional self-loving infant
were three words
I
don't
care
and I am an inferior preacher.

Beth Goodwill (14)
West Somerset Community College, Minehead

Britain

Britain,
An overload in greediness,
Selfishness,
And no concern for others.

We sit back and watch people starve,
Watch them until they cannot move,
Let absolute poverty wipe out so many people,
Unknown to our terrible rate of obesity,
Find it hard to give or share,
Whilst generous charities work until dawn to help.

Teenagers wandering streets at midnight,
Smoking,
Causing disruption,
Oblivious to their health problems,
And we just let them.

The Prime Minister,
Scared of being found out,
The mysterious death of Doctor David Kelly,
Lying,
Cheating,
Killing people before they have already gone to war.

Britain,
Lying to itself,
Unable to find truth,
Help themselves,
Keep to the law,
Is it just a scam of its own?

Emily Townsend (14)
West Somerset Community College, Minehead

Talkin' 'Bout My Generation

Being a teenager,
In a school made of pieces,
Like a jigsaw puzzle,
All put together.

Chavs, jocks, Goths,
All one big family,
Plastics, nerds and outcasts,
Add to the quantity.

In our world,
It's hard to cope,
So much pressure,
But so little support.

Gaining friends,
Is never easy,
When,
You're all torn between.

Gossip is like butter,
Easy to spread,
But bitter to taste

It's hard to fit in,
When you're not so thin,
And it's hard to feel pretty,
When you're seen as ugly.

I've leant to hold on,
To my individuality,
There's only one of me
And that's the way it should be.

If someone tries,
To put you down,
Just walk on by,
Don't turn around,
You only have to answer to yourself.

You know,
It's true what they say,
Life, it ain't easy,
But there's only going to be,
One generation,
Just like ours.

Take it by storm,
Let it run wild,
Give it all you've got
And never regret.

Michelle Saunders
West Somerset Community College, Minehead

All Kids Need Is . . .

N eed it to fuel our developing lives,
I ndependent and grouped work,
C an't go without it,
K nowledge is key to success.

H appy days,
O utside or inside we don't care,
S o many words and different aspects,
E ngage our brains,
G iving a world of opportunities,
O nly dedication is accepted,
O nly practise will suffice,
D etails are analysed for improvement,

S imple or sophisticated,
A ll day or in doses,
Y es children do love it,
S urprised.

We do love our . . . sport,
What did you think I was talking about?
Education,
We don't need that, give us sport and we will be fine.

Nick Hosegood (14)
West Somerset Community College, Minehead

Teenagers

B eing a teenager is a constant challenge,
E verything is stacked against us,
I n lessons, for forgetting homework,
N ope, it's just not fair,
G oing home is more trouble, a bus to catch, a bag to carry,

A nd it doesn't stop there,

T ormenting teachers,
E xhausting lessons,
E xams and tests,
N o way of getting out of it,
A lright, it's not that hard, ha, ha,
G reat sense of humour as well,
E verything is still stacked against us,
R eally it's not our fault we're teenagers.

Jacob Cammidge
West Somerset Community College, Minehead

The Teenage Poom

Some teenagers are mature,
Some teenagers are immature,
Some teenagers are rich,
Some teenagers are poor,
They come in different shapes and sizes,
Some are tall,
Some are small,
A teenager's at least thirteen,
A teenager is tall and lean,
Teenagers like having a laugh,
But when sweaty, they need a bath,
I am a teenager and thirteen,
I'm also skinny, tall and lean.

Connor Murphy (13)
West Somerset Community College, Minehead

Teenager Means Freedom!

Teenager means freedom,
With a few restrictions,
Still living with Mum,
Afraid of Big Brother eviction.

But it's not all that great,
Sometimes I'm confused,
Falling out with my best mate,
Messing up my life to my later fate.

People should get on,
There is no need for murder,
Also no need for a can,
Finish the stereotyping.

Freedom is great like the sun,
Love glows like a fire,
Always time for the fun,
No need for a liar.

Harry Mouzouri
West Somerset Community College, Minehead

Talkin' 'Bout My Generation

Do you know what it is like to be a teenager in 2007?
I do because I am,
I'm 13,
And I am a boy.

Everything changes,
People become chavs and others become Goths,
You make new friends
And old ones leave you.

Just me and my mates want to have fun,
Playing our games,
Football, rugby, basketball and just going out on our bikes.

Greg Wood (13)
West Somerset Community College, Minehead

Untitled

Fun, laughter, having good times,
Chilling on the beach pumpin' some rhymes,
Drinking some booze,
Getting drunk with your mates,
Getting in relationships, going on dates,
Having some sex, having a buzz,
Getting away from parents,
Who do make a fuss.

Playing some sport, stuck in a hole,
I hate those little gits, who are on the dole,
I drown bad memories and put them in a jar,
I go down the stream and cast them afar.

Life's a bitch. Nuff said.

Dean Manley (13)
West Somerset Community College, Minehead

Talkin' 'Bout My Generation

Being a teenager isn't always cruising,
You can sometimes get a bruising,
It's not easy,
Sometimes it can be crazy,
It's hard,
It's tough,
And it can be very rough,
But it can be lovely,
And can be very odd,
So if I were you,
Make the most of your teen life.

Bradley Price (13)
West Somerset Community College, Minehead

Teenage Questionnaire

What makes you angry?
Is it your small brothers or sisters
Or is it cause you get blamed for something
You didn't do and that is why we always feel angry?
What makes you happy?
It is when you can get out of school for the weekend,
Or is it doing whatever you want to, whenever you want?
What's the best thing about being a teenager?
Is it that you get to go out whenever you want,
Or could it be that you get to make your own decision?
What makes you a teenager?

Ryan Lewis & Jack Coward
West Somerset Community College, Minehead

My Poem

Make-up, oh make-up,
What a wonderful fix up,
How I would love to put on the lot.

Foundation to blusher to
Mascara, here we go,
From ugly to stunner,
With it on, I look like a princess
But without it on,
I look like an ugly princess.

Make-up, oh make-up.

Christina Le Rendu
West Somerset Community College, Minehead

Talkin' 'Bout My Generation

School - it's a drag,
Am lost in a machine,
Home - it's a hole,
A place to rest my head,
Girls - where do I start?
They're a mystery to me.

Pressure - lots of peer pressure.
From all my friends,
Sport - what a great thing,
Awesome to everyone,
Clothes - some chavy, some gothic,
But who cares what you wear.

Parents - greatest thing ever,
Just for children,
Future - what will happen?
Where will we go?
War - guns, death and crime,
All it is is a waste of time.

Joe Francis
West Somerset Community College, Minehead

Livin' It Up!

Staying up late partyin',
Goin' out with mates,
There's more to bein' a teenager,
There's good times and bad!
Happy times and sad,
Funny times and scary,
But you'll always be havin' fun,
I swear,
When you're annoyed,
Just sit back and say,
I'm a teenager and I rock!
Nobody will listen,
But it's better than bein' a kid,
You'd better enjoy bein' a teenager,
Cause,
It's the best time of your life,
Live it to the full,
Test the limits,
And love every second of it.

Annie Rowling
West Somerset Community College, Minehead

Teenagers

Who are we?
We are normal teenagers,
We don't drink under age,
We don't smoke under age,
We don't take drugs,
We don't vandalise.

What do we do?
We go to school,
We do exams,
We do homework.

What are our hopes?
To pass exams,
To get a job,
To learn to drive.

What annoys us?
Having to go to school,
Having to do homework so we can't do
What we want to do,
Having pressure put on us.

Katherine Peeks (14)
West Somerset Community College, Minehead

Teenage Life!

Life is great!
When you're a teenager, life is *amazing*!
The only problem is when you are angry,
Just when people boss you around,
When you fight with people,
But don't worry it will get sorted out,
Most of the time, I'm happy, lively, crazy and hyper,
Oh the joys of being a teenager,
Some of us are affected by peer pressure,
Some into alcohol and drugs,
Teenage life is fun, life just gets better and better,
You can do more things than when you were a few years younger,
You hope that everything will get better as life goes on,
When things go wrong, that's the only thing to worry about
But you'll get it sorted,
People think that we are misunderstood
I don't think many are!
I'm sure not!
There is nothing to worry about,
Life is great when you are a teenager.

Faye Wolley (13)
West Somerset Community College, Minehead

What A Teenage Outcast

From the studded belt,
To the spiked up hair,
I know what they think,
But I try not to care.

From all the rumours,
And all the lies,
They tease and torment,
Never caring who cries.

I hate them so much,
For all that they have done,
They do it on purpose,
I just want to run.

Run home to the music,
My own little world,
Look deeper inside,
The story unfurls.

But you can't look deeper,
To you there's nothing to see,
They say it's skin deep,
But that's just not me.

The school, the friends,
The boys, the tears,
The head in the hands,
The screams no one hears.

Go ahead, do it,
Turn back if you dare,
But to me,
I'd go anywhere but there.

Eleanor Facey (13)
West Somerset Community College, Minehead

Young Writers Information

We hope you have enjoyed reading this book - and that you will continue to enjoy it in the coming years.

If you like reading and writing poetry drop us a line, or give us a call, and we'll send you a free information pack.

Alternatively if you would like to order further copies of this book or any of our other titles, then please give us a call or log onto our website at www.youngwriters.co.uk

**Young Writers Information
Remus House
Coltsfoot Drive
Peterborough
PE2 9JX**

(01733) 890066